Amy Knapp's
Family
Organizing
Handbook

314 Mom-Tested Super Tips, Tricks and Secrets to
TAKE CARE OF EVERYTHING WITH TIME LEFT FOR WHAT REALLY MATTERS

by Amy Knapp

SOURCEBOOKS, INC.®
NAPERVILLE, ILLINOIS

Published by Sourcebooks, Inc.
P.O. Box 4410, Naperville, Illinois 60567–4410
(630) 961–3900
Fax: (630) 961–2168
www.sourcebooks.com

Library of Congress Cataloging-in-Publication Data

Knapp, Amy.
  [Family organizing handbook]
  Amy Knapp's family organizing handbook : 314 mom-tested super tips,
tricks, and secrets to take care of everything with time left for what really
matters / by Amy Knapp.
      p. cm.
  Includes bibliographical references and index.
  ISBN-13: 978-1-4022-0761-7 (alk. paper)
  ISBN-10: 1-4022-0761-1 (alk. paper)
  1. Family—Time management. 2. Mothers—Time management. 3.
House cleaning. 4. Parenting. I. Title. II. Title: Family organizing handbook.

HQ734.K653 2006
640—dc22

2006019059

Printed and bound in the United States of America
CHG 10 9 8 7 6 5 4 3 2 1

To my children, Kyle and Natalie, who make me want to be a better person. And to my husband, Dave, who makes me that better person. All my love and thanks for your unwavering support.

Acknowledgments

I never thought I would write a book. And frankly, without the support of many people, it probably would not have happened—and certainly would not have been so pleasurable an experience. I must first thank Sourcebooks for the opportunity. The entire organization has been incredibly encouraging, patient, and enthusiastic. I hate to single out one or two people, but I must…the very talented Susie Benton took the chaos I actually called a manuscript and edited it into a document with wonderful flow without losing the function. Deb and Dominique, your belief in me was often stronger than my belief in myself. Thank you for your support.

My heart spoke about my family in the dedication, but I must thank them again for all their love, support, and willingness to order pizza again! Lastly, but certainly not least, I want to thank all the women—moms, grandmas, and thirty-somethings—who have purchased organizers and many of whom have taken the time to contact me with words of encouragement, stories of perseverance, and ideas for improvement. Their timing is always perfect. Many hard, discouraging, stressful days were brightened by a few kind, supportive words. There are so many to thank, but please know that I feel truly blessed to have been given the life experiences that put me in the position to write this book.

TABLE OF CONTENTS

Introduction

After I became a full-time, stay-at-home Mom, I struggled to get my family organized. I had been a successful businesswoman and, with the birth of my son Kyle, a working Mom—and very thankful for both of these very challenging and rewarding roles.

In 1995 our daughter Natalie was born and within two months was hospitalized with meningitis. (There is nothing like sleeping on a hospital couch for a week to make you re-evaluate your priorities.) When Natalie was nine months old, it became apparent that there were long-term medical complications from the meningitis, so I decided to sell out of my business and join the ranks of stay-at-home mothers. It was a decision my family and I have never regretted.

I was amazed, however, by my lack of productivity after just a short time at home with the kids. I had always been a self-starter, but I couldn't seem to get it going at home, let alone keep it running smoothly. Being an avid business planner geek, I was very frustrated with the various products for keeping track of appointments, errands, and schedules, none of which were working for me in my new role at home. This frustration led me to create my own organizer. It wasn't fancy, but it worked, and soon my friends and other moms I encountered began asking me to make one for them. That early prototype became *Amy Knapp's Family Organizer*, which I have been blessed to be able to share with hundreds of thousands of women across the country.

Natalie is doing great, enjoying her therapeutic horseback riding and learning and growing each day. Kyle has turned me into a full-fledged football-baseball-wrestling-golf Mom as he dives deeper each year into his sports activities. My husband Dave and I recently built a new home and moved the family in. Creating, marketing, and selling *Amy Knapp's Family Organizer* is a wonderful diversion for me from the everyday activities around the house. With the advantage of being able to work from home, my part-time diversion has turned into a full-time adventure, which I can still work around carpooling and all the other family needs. The organizer is the major tool in keeping me organized enough to meet all of my responsibilities at home and work, while still enjoying life—and keeping my family from hating me too much for being a crazy lady! (We call those moments "Ugly Mom.")

The idea for this book was born a couple of years ago when I was doing a weekly email I called the "Weekly Challenge." The email was inspired by my Grandma Ruth and went out to thousands of women. We all tackled the same task each week. When you are at home every day doing many of the same things over and over, it can feel a little lonely (even if your house is full of little feet). There was something supportive about knowing that other women around the country were cleaning the bugs out of their light fixtures right along with you!

As with any change or improvement we consider, the first important question to ask, of course, is "why"? Why be organized? Well, what I've found in my own life—that's been borne out by hundreds and even thousands of things I've heard from my customers over the years—is that being more organized frees me up for what really matters in my life. Getting my household to function efficiently has allowed me to feel more confident as a wife and mother, given me more time to be involved at my kids' schools, pursue a Bible study class that enriches me personally, share more quality time with my husband, and myriad activities large and small that my family and I enjoy and that allow us to bond, to enjoy each other, and to grow.

Our family has recently had the exciting experience of building a house—or, I should say more accurately, watching it be built. There were so many decisions to be made—do you want one towel bar or two? Brushed nickel or polished chrome? Despite all these details, as our move-in date approached, it seemed that something very important was missing. Our "dream" house was very beautiful, but not quite as dreamy as I thought. I realized my dream was not about a structure, but about a family. How do you take four walls and a roof and make it a home? Not just a structure filled with furniture and your personal possessions, but a safe, comfortable, functional environment for people (and pets!), each one bringing their own set of expectations and personal preferences, not to mention their busy schedules. I realized a beautifully functional family home was my dream! An environment where the vivid memories from our old house of first steps and lost teeth could be replaced by sleepovers and first dates.

In the process of moving our possessions in, I was reminded again that a home really has little to do with the physical things in it. You can hang family pictures and display keep-sakes, which will create a sense of familiarity, but a home is really defined by how your family functions within that space. Material things aside, a comfortable home is one that functions on a daily basis with the least amount of chaos!

The tips and associated tasks included in this book come both from my personal experience, and input from women around the country. It didn't take me long in my new venture to realize what motivated and encouraged me. I loved hearing from other moms and found their approaches to parenting and homemaking so enlightening and refreshing, I put a survey on my website to encourage more targeted interaction. I was not disappointed. I have included (with consent) some of these honest, funny, and encouraging comments, as well as some organizing tips from the front lines. Some of these tips are fresh new ideas, and others are tried and true techniques that it never hurts to be reminded of.

I've included a number of fun reminders for commonly overlooked areas of the house, places where you can apply special attention and reap big rewards. My Grandma Ruth was a remarkable housekeeper. You would never have found bugs in her light fixtures or three bottles of half-used dish soap under her kitchen sink. Although she lived in a different time, when there were not five baseball and/or softball games in a week, two hours of homework each night, and thirty-five emails requiring reply every morning, I feel that she had the right idea, one that we can still learn from. If you pay due attention to the little things in life and at home, the big stuff seems to fall into place. On the contrary, if you concentrate only on the big stuff, the little things will always remain unfinished or overlooked, and can lead to more stress than you might imagine or want. How simple, but challenging. It seems to go against our very fibers: we get so used to putting things off, doing what has to get done, and sweeping the rest under the rug. But after a while, that doesn't feel so good.

In this book I'm going to draw upon all the wonderfully unique, creative, and resourceful people I have met—in person or electronically—in the course of my "Weekly Challenge," other writing and publishing projects, and everyone else who has blessed my daily life. I love opening an email and reading how a mom from Iowa solved a laundry problem in a practical way. It may seem like a little thing, but those little things can add up to huge timesavings and go a long way toward having a home that runs more smoothly. Notice my choice of words: *more* smoothly...*less* chaos. There is never going to be a home that runs *perfectly* smoothly or has *no* chaos—not in this life, anyway. Once we have set realistic expectations and begin to work toward them, we have taken the hardest, most important step in creating and maintaining a comfortable home.

And that, fundamentally, is what this book is about: your family's comfort and enjoyment—the ease with which chores get done, routines that make everyone's life simpler, more time to spend together, and more time to relax. A little bit of organizing can go a long way toward this goal. And along the way, I wish you to celebrate your small successes, learn from your big mistakes—and laugh at all the rest.

Getting in Touch with
Your Inner Organizer

*O*ver the years, I have noticed that there are certain personal traits associated with being more organized than the general population. They are common threads that, by themselves and in conjunction with one another, set the stage for a lifestyle that incorporates being organized as second nature and allows you to achieve more and work less.

Being organized requires you to focus both on the big picture and the little pieces that make it up. It is like putting together a jigsaw puzzle. You really have to look at and examine each piece to see what it looks like. What are the colors and the shape? Is it a corner piece? But no matter how hard you study the piece, you will not know where it goes without considering what the puzzle is supposed to look like complete; the big picture. Our lives are like a huge, never-ending puzzle. We get a few pieces at a time. If you can look at a task, see where it fits in, and concentrate on the reward instead of dreading the process, life is a joy.

KNOW YOURSELF (FORGET ABOUT PERFECTION HERE)

You will have the greatest propensity to be organized if you have realistic expectations of yourself, others, and the world around you. After all, how much time do you want to spend trying to put a square peg into a round hole?

It's best to be honest with yourself about who you are and what your limitations are. You need to know when to push yourself and when to pull back. It is not a matter of who you want to be, but of understanding and being comfortable with who you are right now. Small, gradual changes can take hold, but vast reinventions rarely last and break down our self-confidence along the way.

In the next section I talk about knowing your organizational style. To really know your own style you must be honest with yourself, otherwise you just try to take on someone else's style, and that doesn't work. If you have a hard time seeing yourself objectively, review your past history. Actions speak louder than words. What situations are you most comfortable in? Which are the most challenging? What is important to you and what is less so? Do you love to entertain and want a pristine living room where adults can relax over cocktails, or are you just as happy sitting on the floor amidst happy children and a pile of toys? Do you have a home-based business and need a clear entryway for packages and deliveries, or are you more concerned about everyone being able to find two matching boots as they race out the door in the morning? Is it essential to you that your bedroom be a peaceful oasis, or are your exercise equipment or hobby supplies more important to your functioning in that room?

As you contemplate the many tips and tasks I'll be sharing with you, take only the ones that appeal to you, that make sense, that sound as though they'll make your life that much better. Anything that sounds too difficult, impractical, anxiety-producing, or downright overwhelming, isn't for you at this time.

But maybe as you contemplate it, you'll have an idea for your own family that will make a great difference. Or maybe you'll come up with a variation that suits your family to a "T" (and maybe you'll be generous and share it with me on my website, www.familyorganizer.com). In short, while I can tell you with great clarity what works and doesn't work for me and my family, I leave it to you to determine what's best for you and yours.

Everything in this book is in service of you and your family's unique style, so begin by being very clear about what matters to you most, and then take it from there.

A Word about Discipline

To be as organized as you can be, you're going to need to be a little tenacious and determined. You're going to develop almost a boomerang quality. You can be drawn away from a task or goal, for either a long or short length of time, but you can always come back to it. This is important because sometimes life can seem to be just a series of interruptions and as one unfinished task piles up on another, it's all too easy to get overwhelmed and throw organization out the window. But, if you're keeping your expectations realistic, and you're clear about what's really important to you, you'll "boomerang" right back to the place you were just before you were interrupted, and carry on from there. You may fall behind sometimes, but you'll never get too far off track and you won't despair or give up, because as you begin to enjoy the fruits of being organized, you're not going to want to go back to the stress of disorganization.

Multitasking vs. Distractions

There is a fine line between multitasking and letting distractions sabotage your productivity. What is the difference? Multitasking is a deliberate decision to accomplish two or more things at one time that do not interfere with effectively and efficiently completing either task. Whenever you compromise the latter part of that definition, you have crossed the line from multitasking to distraction. Talking on the phone while you are emptying the dishwasher is multitasking. Realizing you have been holding the same cup or plate for ten minutes is a sign of distraction.

Remember that boomerang! If you do get distracted, just go right back to the first unfinished task, or wherever you are in your process, and pick up from there.

So as you contemplate the ebb and flow of your busy life and begin the process of getting organized so you can free yourself up for more

Your Inner Organizer

fun and family time, you'll begin to create the structures and processes that you'll want to use and rely upon. You can add layers of detail later, once you have successfully incorporated changes into your lifestyle. For now, keep things ridiculously simple. Remember: you want to celebrate your small successes, learn from your mistakes, and laugh at the rest. Putting calculated, incremental expectations on yourself and your family will allow you to make more time for what really matters…and enjoy it more.

As much as possible, have the individual ideas fit within an existing part of your current infrastructure so you aren't facing an endless list of tasks, but locating yourself within a process so you can pick up right there without stress. And it's easier to get the whole family involved in a process than it is to try to get someone to perform a single task. Everyone participates and has their role—and you know what they say about many hands making light work! Beyond being lighter work, involvement will produce "buy in" from your family. Buy in will result in long-term support for the process and the individual tasks will begin to take care of themselves.

YOUR ORGANIZATIONAL STYLE

We all have unique social personalities: some of us talk a lot, other are quiet, some have a dry sense of humor, others *no* sense of humor at all. We are all different and what works for one person may not work for another. So, too, are our organizational styles unique. There is no one-size-fits-all approach to getting and staying organized.

If you want to know your organizational style, the first place to look is how you keep and maintain your calendar. If you are detail driven, you probably not only start out color-coding your calendar for each family member, but maintain it throughout the entire year. A person that is general but thorough when it comes to organizing probably lasted a couple weeks the first time they attempted the color-coding thing but found searching for the right colored pen more stressful than taking a couple of extra seconds to look at who had the dentist appointment. A generally organized person throws all the kids in the car knowing that one of them has a dentist appointment and actually manages to get there on time! The truly unorganized person misses the appointment altogether and does not realize it until three weeks later because they have yet to purchase their calendar for the year even though it is March. Do you see yourself in one of these?

Believe it or not, there is really only one dysfunctional style above—the truly unorganized.

Each of the other styles can work, understanding that getting organized is the process not the result. The result of being organized should be a decrease in you and your family's stress level and an increase in productivity throughout your home and your life. Think of an old-fashioned weight scale. With no organizational strategies, the balance between effort and results is way off. The idea is to add organizational strategies only to that point where the scales level off! Not enough organization and you are causing yourself and your family undue stress. Too much organization, and you are putting unnecessary pressure on yourself and your family to maintain a system that may be more than your family actually needs. Remember, the goal is to get and stay organized at a level that allows *your* family to function at its highest level of efficiency with the minimum amount of work. Find what is comfortable for you and works for your family. Do not worry about trying to keep up with anyone else or adapt to their style.

Remember our friend who writes each person's activities on the calendar in a different color? It would probably drive her nuts and cause more stress if she did not maintain her system. She draws comfort from the structure rather than being overwhelmed by the detail. Most people I meet or correspond with usually assume that I am a detail-driven person. Actually, I am very general but thorough when it comes to organizing. It works for me and my family. Expertise comes not in perfect execution, but in a thorough understanding of the big picture. Let's face it, running a household with a busy family requires all of us to be experts in our home environment!

The ultimate goal of any organizing system is to decrease stress and get more done with less effort. As we look at our organizational styles, we should strive for the highest level that would not add additional stress. How does your scale look?

ORGANIZING VS. CLEANING

There are books about organizing and books about cleaning. There are products that clean and products that organize. I am not sure how these two concepts ever got such separate identities. Organizing is just a good old-fashioned deep cleaning! The word organizing itself sounds more intimidating than cleaning. If someone says, "I am going to organize my closet," what picture pops into your head? Clothes piled on the bed, a sea of shoes on the floor, hangers jumbled up in a knot. I don't know about you, but I am scared before I even begin.

Cleaning is a mandatory periodic task that needs to be done at some level. Let's approach organizing the same way. If we can clean as we go along, why not organize as we go along? Take five extra minutes today and pull the extra hangers out of your closet. Go through the papers on your desk while you are on the phone. I am very blessed to have Vanessa who helps me clean my house every two weeks. She is wonderful, but she would kill me if I did not do any maintenance between her visits. Can you imagine! How is it we will go a couple of weeks or months putting no effort towards organizing? And then we wonder how we lost control.

I am encouraging you to change how you think about organizing. Change can be a very good productive process; it is a great opportunity to improve on the current status. Consider organizing as part of your standard operating procedure, not an additional task that needs to be done when the ship is sinking. Challenge yourself to be creative in solving your biggest organizing challenges, then share that idea with a friend. Get your kids and family involved. Solve the problems together in a way that accommodates everyone's expectations and limitations. If you want your family to participate in the maintenance, you must get them to buy in up front!

TAKING CARE OF BUSINESS: PLANNING AND SCHEDULING

I have always thought of my brain as a little computer with a finite amount of memory. When I was younger, my brain had 4 GB's of memory, and I could not have filled it all if I tried (which, of course, I didn't). Today, I feel like a dinosaur computer operating on the

Your Inner Organizer

DOS system with only 512K of memory. To compensate for this state of gradual reverse evolution, I need to write everything down.

The real trick is not writing it down, but remembering to look at it. You need to build a confidence level that will allow you to let it go once you've written something down in your organizer or calendar. If you do not use your organizer consistently, you will always feel like you need to hold those appointments in the back of your mind. If you *do* learn to trust yourself and can rely on your system, you'll experience the most wonderful sense of freedom and lightness.

Following is everything you need to know to get started on a life of uncluttered mental capacities. These tips will show you how to create good habits for yourself, keep running to-do lists that allow for both long-term and short-term accomplishments, set triggers for yourself to help you plan ahead, and be proactive for upcoming obligations and events. I recently was late for an appointment because, although I had reviewed my calendar the night before, by morning I had somehow gotten it into my head that the appointment was at 10:00 a.m. when in fact it was at 9:00. My usual quick check in the morning would have eliminated the mistake. Lesson learned—continually reinforce your good habits.

Unclutter Your Head

This is not a new concept, but one of the biggest keys to getting and staying organized is to reduce clutter. There are two types of clutter: physical and mental. In chapter 4, I'll give you plenty of ideas for dealing with physical clutter. Mental clutter is less apparent, but can be double the trouble. We have all been there; paralyzed by the feeling of being overwhelmed emotionally and mentally. You cannot take in one more thing. Well, the best way to control mental clutter is to write things down in an organized way.

1 **Use an organizer, calendar, or journal to keep track of important dates and appointments.** This is key, and we'll talk about how to coordinate your personal organizer with the family calendar in chapter 2.

2 **Take your organizer with you whenever possible and check it often.**

3 **Use this same tool to write down important information you want to remember,** so you don't have to try to hold it in your short-term memory. Highlight it so that you can find it quickly when you need to refer back to it!

What's the Plan?

Which Came First, the Chicken or the Egg?

In an ideal world, you would take ten to fifteen minutes each morning in a quiet, uninterrupted place to firm up your plans for the day and look over the next few days. Okay, is everyone saying, "Quiet? Uninterrupted? Have you seen my house?" It's the old Chicken and Egg debate. Which comes first: the organized house that makes it easier to keep the routine, or the routine that organizes your schedule and your house? Look at it this way; the house is not going to magically organize itself, and we have to start somewhere—usually from where we are. If your life is feeling chaotic, what do you have to lose by taking a little time to make it better?

4 **Create a routine for reviewing your calendar and to-do list.** It can (and must) be what works for you; the important thing is to get it going.

5 If first thing in the morning just doesn't work, what about a midmorning coffee break to look over your schedule and get you sailing through the next twenty-four hours? It can be after lunch or after midnight, **as long as you do it regularly and it works for you.**

Out of Your Head and Into Your Plan: Appointments

Phone calls are easy to make and can take very little time. So why is that we put them off with such consistency? Maybe it's because we try to put too much in our memory and not enough in our schedule.

6 **Go through and think about any appointments or meetings you have been putting off.** Make a list and download it all from your brain. Has your six-month dental checkup surpassed annual status? Is retirement creeping closer and closer and you still have not completed your New Year's resolution from two years ago—to meet with a financial advisor? Why not be early for next year's mammogram, since you put this year's off for eleven months?

7 **Warning, if you sit down to get caught up on all these appointments, do not try to schedule everything for the same week.** Spread them out, otherwise you will end up feeling overwhelmed!

8 **Take as much time as you think is appropriate,** but be sure to actually schedule everything into your calendar or organizer. Then you can stop worrying about them.

9 If the day of your dental checkup approaches and **it's impossible to make the appointment, reschedule immediately** and save yourself the mental anguish of putting it back on your to-do list.

Getting It All Handled

Keep a running long-term and short-term to-do list in a central location or permanently with your calendar so you will always know where to find it.

10 **On the short-term list include those tasks and items that need to be completed in the next week or two.**

11 **Prioritize the items using a letter or number system or even a highlighter.** Figure out how much time—either all at once or in smaller increments—you will need to complete the task.

12 **Schedule time on your calendar for your high priority items.**

13 Now look at the next level of tasks. **Can you piggyback them to accomplish two things at once?** Can you call the doctor on your way to pick up the dry cleaning? Pay bills while you are waiting for practice to end?

14

Cross off items as they are completed. Don't skip this step—it's amazing how rewarding and satisfying it is. You might want to have a special pen for the purpose, in your favorite bright color of ink.

15

On your long-term to-do list, put items that are either farther off or require a greater time commitment. Write a regular appointment in your weekly schedule to work on these long-term projects/goals, and you won't have to have them constantly weighing on you the rest of the time.

Your Calendar Works Hard—So You Don't Have To

I have learned that I cannot count on myself to remember things, but seeing it on paper makes it more concrete. I may tell myself I need to call the airline this week and book a flight, but if I do not write it down, it is at high risk of being forgotten or put off indefinitely. It is much easier to put off something when you haven't really made a formal commitment to doing it by putting it in your schedule.

16 **As you are writing an appointment on your calendar, write the contact phone number next to it.** If you are running late or need to cancel, you will not have to search for the number.

17 **Planning a spring vacation?** Pick a week in the fall to look into travel plans and write it into your schedule. Do you usually take cupcakes to school for your child's birthday? Add the ingredients you will need to the grocery list the week before.

18 **Using a 3 x 5 index card, create a reusable weekly to-do list,** for example: Monday—clean bathrooms, Tuesday—dust, Wednesday—wash floors. Laminate the card and clip it on your calendar, or keep the card with your organizer and to-do list. As you are making appointments or other commitments, you will have a reminder of the basic tasks you had planned for the day.

Time for Everything

As Moms we wear so many different hats. We are often called upon to change roles mid-sentence without missing a beat. The problem with these quick transformations is that our brains have a hard time catching up. It takes a little preparation to put my brain in "balance the checkbook" mode. If I stop to answer an email or make lunch for the kids, it is hard to regain the momentum I had when I left.

19 **Schedule blocks of time in your day for specific activities.** For example: return phone calls from 9:00 to 9:30, respond to emails from 10:00 to 10:30, do a quick pick up around the house from 4:00 to 4:30. There are many things that will require your immediate response, but establishing a daily schedule will help keep small things from falling through the cracks. Make sure to schedule a realistic amount of time.

It's Your Plan, and You Can Change It

As the day progresses, you get busy and outside influences intrude, it is easy to overlook things that may have a deadline or that someone else is counting on your doing. We have all dropped the ball (some of us more than once) and know how terrible that moment of truth feels. While your to-do list should act as

Your Inner Organizer

your map as you navigate your day, circumstances and priorities change consistently. You need to be able to react and adjust. Of course, to make calculated adjustments you need to know what you are dealing with.

When looking at your to-do list, be honest with yourself. Which items are a *have to* and which are a *want to*? Differentiate and set your schedule and day with the *have to*'s at the top of the list. Often the *want to*'s are the reward for getting those other things done. In a crunch situation, or when emotions take over, *want to*'s can seem like *have to*'s, especially if you haven't sorted them out at the start.

20 Take a few minutes each evening or first thing in the morning to identify those tasks that are high priority for the coming day. Make these the cornerstones of your day.

21 **As you check your to-do list, cross off what you have completed and review what still needs to be done.** Consider how to work remaining tasks into your schedule most efficiently.

22 **Re-evaluate your list throughout the day.** Decide if any priorities have changed. Is picking up the dry cleaning less important because you just picked up your sick child from school and will not be attending the function tonight that you needed the dress for?

23 **Give yourself a break.** Going to the grocery store may seem like a *have to*, but on the day when nothing went right, maybe an adjustment in your menu, using ingredients on hand, is a better

solution. Sure, you *wanted to* have the particular dish you were planning, but in the end, is it really worth the additional stress?

24 **When you make these necessary adjustments to your daily priorities and list, reset your success meter to that point.** Do not look back and beat yourself up because the original plan did not work out!

Is It Worth It?

The whole point of organizing your home and your schedule is to have time for what really matters to you and your family, right? It's easy to get bogged down in the task at hand, especially when there's so much you want to do. It's a good idea to re-evaluate from time to time how you are spending your time! Alphabetizing the spice rack may be fun, but if it is taking time away from playing with your kids, or helping down at the church, or—you name it—do you want to take it off your to-do list and learn to live with less well-organized spices?

25 **Periodically, take an objective look at your calendar, schedule, and to-do list.** Can you identify any time wasters? Are you spending more time on certain activities or tasks than they are worth in terms of the bigger picture?

The Well-Oiled Machine:
Getting Everyone on the Same Track

Did you ever play the game "telephone" when you were young? Even if you did not have a bunch of smart alecks playing, it was difficult to get a consistent message passed through even a few people. The reason: people bring their own perspectives—based on personality, age, and life experiences—into everything they do. Four people living under one roof surely will have similar perspectives—NOT. If your family is like mine, there is only one correct perspective—mine—and I spend most of my time trying to convince the rest of them to come over to my side. Only kidding (most of the time), but sometimes I do feel as though I am swimming upstream! That's when I realize that I have forgotten to *include* my family and everything they bring into the process.

The good news: it is never too late to get them involved. By involved, I am not just talking about physical involvement—more important is their emotional and intellectual involvement. The value of effective communication and complete involvement is amazing. Less complaining, less nagging. More hands, lighter loads. More minds, better solutions. All of this translates into less stress and more time for what really matters!

THE FAMILY CALENDAR: YOUR CENTRAL COMMUNICATION TOOL

Let's start with the family calendar. The family calendar is the most important tool in the house, especially a household with growing kids. Multiple work, school, and home schedules make it essential to have one central calendar that everyone uses as the master schedule.

When it comes to calendars, people tend to divide into two camps: wall versus desk planner. The truth is, they should complement one another, not compete. When my children were younger, scheduling was much less complicated; not that we had fewer commitments and were less busy, but the kids were not as actively involved. Frankly, they went where I told them they were going—ah, the good old days. Some days, my husband still thinks he is on that plan.

Back then, as long as we actively communicated, my trusty organizer was all we needed to keep all of us on track. Now, I still live by my organizer, but a wall calendar has replaced it as the central family scheduler. This is in a handy location where everyone can consult and update it.

There are a few tricks to making this process run smoothly for everyone—as with most tools, a calendar or organizer is only as good as its users. Double booking an afternoon is never the calendar's fault! But once everyone gets used to maintaining the family calendar, you'll be amazed how much easier life becomes.

26 Put the family calendar in a highly visible location.

27 Assign a family member to be the calendar's gatekeeper. If both parents work outside the home, they will

probably share in this responsibility; otherwise the job usually goes to the parent who is home the most. The gatekeeper's job is to monitor what is going onto and coming off the calendar, to keep an eye out for potential conflicts, and to communicate with the rest of the family.

28 **Keep it neat.** Write fixed events and special dates such as birthdays and anniversaries in pen or marker. Write everything else in pencil to allow for the schedule changes that are sure to come with a busy family. If you color code your calendar by family member, you will need to use colored pencils, or learn to live with some crossed out entries.

29

Train the kids. Access and responsibility will increase as they get older and eventually begin to coordinate with their own organizers or planners. At first, the family calendar should be for younger kids to look at only. Using stickers or pictures is a great way to engage the very young. As your children begin to write legibly, help them to write their own activities on the calendar. They'll find this to be fun, and it is good training for when they start using their own organizer. In the beginning (and actually for quite a while), you will want to closely supervise as entries are made to the family calendar by younger family members, making sure they are put on the right date and do not conflict with any previous commitments. Nothing is to be erased or crossed out without the gatekeeper's approval.

30 **Synchronize.** I love to have things down on paper, especially my calendar—looking at a little screen with dots that tell me I have a commitment that day drives me nuts—but with the paper habit comes a little extra effort.

On paper, you cannot update entries with the push of a button or just by walking into the room, so you have to train yourself to update the family calendar from your portable organizer. The organizer is great because it allows you space for more detailed planning and you can take it with you to appointments and meetings, which result in further scheduling or other follow-up commitments. Keep the family calendar uncluttered by entering just the basics—who, what, when, and where.

31 **Review.** There is a Catch-22 when it comes to writing things down on our calendars. You write it down so that you do not have to hold it in your immediate memory, but that means you are dependent on the calendar to remember it. Review your calendar every night before bed and then again in the morning to make sure you know the day's commitments, and train/coach your family to do the same.

32 **Communicate.** The family calendar should not replace verbal communication within the family; it should complement and confirm it. Make sure that everyone in the family knows that it is dangerous to assume that everyone else has checked and understands the schedule. Weekly family meetings on Sunday night are a great way to make sure the whole family is starting their week out with a common under-standing of the upcoming schedule.

Taking Messages

Another useful tool for good communication is the family message log. Use a notebook or pad of paper to create a log for phone messages and conversation notes.

33 **When you are taking a message** for another family member, whether listening to the answering machine or speaking with someone on the phone, record the message including: date and time, who it is for, who it is from, a return phone number, and a brief explanation if possible.

34 As messages are reviewed, have family members check them off.

35 If there is something that needs immediate attention, flag it, or otherwise draw attention to it so that its recipient can respond.

36 Use the family message log to jot down notes, phone numbers, names, and dates while you are **talking on the phone** (as long as the information is not private or privileged). You will know where to look when you need to retrieve the information, even months later.

But I'm Upstairs

Cordless phones are great. We can go anywhere

in the house while not missing a beat on the phone. The downside to this versatility is being ready to jot a note or record a phone number. It used to be you could keep supplies close at hand and near the phone. Not such an easy thing when the phone is a moving target.

37 **Stash a pencil and note pad** in a bathroom drawer, in the laundry room cabinet, in your child's playroom, etc., for taking notes on the move.

38 **If you take a message for another family member,** just tear it off the pad and clip it to the family message log. Keep a stash of paper clips by the log for this purpose.

GETTING THE KIDS OFF TO A GOOD START

As parents, we aspire to instill many fine traits in our children: a strong work ethic, respect for others, honesty. All great and essential qualities, but teaching them the value of time management is one of the greatest gifts you can give your children. It is a skill with a lifetime of rewards. As effective time managers, they will be more productive in school and later in their professional and home lives. They will have less stress and a greater sense of direction and accomplishment in their lives. An exaggeration? I personally do not think so.

In a society of procrastinators, we have collectively taught our children to wait until the last minute—after all, they see us practicing this behavior all the time. Who has not run to the local twenty-four-hour superstore to pick up cupcakes for the school party the next day, even though you had known about it for several weeks? Do you consistently run late as a result of procrastination? Kids learn early that this is your family's standard operating procedure. It really isn't that difficult to start them off on the right track, although it may require a little more deliberate thought and action. Always be sure to include plenty of games and rewards in the process (not a bad idea for adults, either).

39 **The first and most important step to helping your children become effective time managers is to set a good example.** Make sure they see how you (and they) benefit when you manage your time. Do your kids see you making deliberate choices instead of reacting to emergencies? Do you allow them to see you prioritizing what needs to get done and setting a plan to accomplish everything? Do they see the benefit when you have time to take them to the lake or just sit down and relax? Take a look from your child's perspective, what do they see? What matters most to them, and how can you assist them to have more time for that?

40 Many parenting books encourage parents to put their newborns on a schedule. Anyone who has raised a toddler knows the benefits of an established afternoon nap. As kids get older, though, we often move away from strict schedules or routines, especially with multiple children. This may be doing the kids a disservice. **Establishing basic routines for even the most ordinary tasks will help kids get things done with less hassle and feel good about themselves, too.** Take a

look at what your kids need to get done in the morning: make their beds, brush their teeth, shower, feed the dog. Whatever their chore list looks like, help them form a productive, time efficient routine. As they practice the routine, it will become habit. (Bad habits we pick up, good habits are intentionally established.)

41 **Always take into account your child's personality in establishing both routines and rewards.** Remember, you are setting your kids up for success, not failure. Personally, I make my bed as soon as I get out of it; this accomplishes two things for me: first, the job is done, and second, I cannot crawl back into it, and there are some cold mornings in Michigan when that sounds pretty good. But this "up and at 'em" routine is not one that would work for my son—he wakes up differently

than I do. He needs time to adjust to the world before he can function.

42 **Help your kids find time for their chores:** for instance, emptying the dishwasher takes them five minutes, feeding the dog takes two minutes. Teach them to efficiently use small segments of downtime to get something done. Again, this skill is most effectively taught when they see you doing it on a regular basis in your own life. As parents, our example has tremendous influence.

43 We have all seen the ten-minute task that turns into a thirty-minute ordeal, with twenty minutes spent dreading and complaining before anything gets started. As adults, we often dread or complain under our breath or in our heads, but kids voice everything. If your child seems to be wasting a lot of time complaining, make a game of it like this: start a stopwatch the next time you ask them to do something. **Time how long they spend complaining, and then how long it actually took to complete the task at hand.** Share your results, stressing how much time was wasted compared to how long the task actually took to accomplish. You might want to try this on yourself as well! Time complaining and dreading could be spent on what matters most! What matters most to you today?

44 **Always make sure that your children's chores are age-appropriate and that they have the training and tools they need to succeed.** Once they succeed, provide a reward—one that makes them feel

On the Same Track

good. Make sure that their reward is not a punishment in disguise! I grew up on a farm. The mudroom was absolutely the worst room in our house to clean. One day I had the solo job of cleaning this troublesome area. It must have been the early organizer coming out in me, but I cleaned and organized that room as close to perfection as any of us had ever seen. I was really proud of myself...and so was my Mom. The downside came when I was assigned the job permanently. Thinking it was a one-time deal, I had set a standard higher than I wanted to maintain!

45

I have seen a trend in schools to provide students with assignment calendars or books. Often they are actually being graded on it! **I recommend you get your kids started using a calendar as**

soon as possible; it is usually predicated by increasing commitments—assignments, practices, dances, etc. All kids should have a solid foundation before going into middle school where they will be required to have more independence and increasing accountability.

46

Check your child's book regularly with them, encouraging them to keep it neat and updated. Sit down together, you with your calendar and them with theirs, and make sure your schedules are synchronized. At the beginning, keeping a calendar is sure to feel like more work with little reward. Your encouragement and support will be critical to keep them going. They will begin to see the benefits when they are not cramming at the last minute for a test or paper, but have more time for what matters most to them. Ask your child today what matters most to them.

Pitching In

This is still a work in progress around our house, but we are trying to teach our kids to see things outside their normal sphere of vision. How kids can step over their own shoes twenty times and never pick them up—or seemingly even see them—is perplexing. The water glass that has been on their nightstand for days might as well be invisible. Teaching them to see that something needs to be done—and act on it—is a major milestone.

47 **The first step is to stop picking up after them.** I know this is hard. I could pick up my son's shoes and put them in his locker without missing a beat and be

done with it. Instead, I will leave the shoes there, ask him to put them away, listen to five minutes of complaining, ask him again, listen to more complaining…eventually the job will be done!

48 **Don't fret, kids do get better at this, but you need to be consistent.** Let it be their responsibility. Each time explain how much easier it is to put things away in the first place. They will eventually catch on!

Many Hands Make Light Work

Use your children's enthusiasm to make a game out of house "work."

49 **Put a pair of old socks on each of their hands.** Give them a set amount of time and see who can come back with the dirtiest socks. Even if their

dusting job isn't perfect, those clean patches will be sure to motivate you to finish the job! And you might want to try the "sock on the hand" bit yourself—why should the kids have all the fun?

Create a Family Chore Grab Bag

50 **Make a list of household chores that can be completed in fifteen minutes or less and are doable by** most, if not all, of your family members.

51 **Write each one of the tasks on a piece of paper or index card.** Fold it, concealing what is written. Put all the items in a large basket, bowl, or bag (creative idea—use a cookie jar on the counter!).

52 **When you find yourself with fifteen minutes to spare or your son wants to earn some extra allowance money or the kids are complaining that they're bored, go to the grab bag!** It is a great way to have the whole family help with chores.

53 A fun twist is to make some of the cards fifteen-minute treats or rewards. You never know what you might draw!

Making Yourself...Expendable

When my children were younger and I had to go out of town, I would try to make things as easy as possible for my husband. He is very supportive and willing to do whatever it takes, but I know it is hard to jump in and take on added responsibilities. It also eased my guilt while I was gone to know I'd done all I could to ensure that things would run smoothly.

54 **To help with the morning routine, take paper grocery bags, one for each child for each day you will be gone.** With a quick check of the weather and a glance at daily activities, you can select appropriate attire for each day. Put everything needed for the day—including underclothing, socks, and hair accessories—in a bag and label it with name and date (i.e. Katie, Monday).

55 **Line up the bags in the order they will be used.** Each morning there will be a bag ready to grab with everything they need to get ready for the day.

56 Set a basket next to the bags with hairbrushes, toothbrushes, and paste, so everything that's used daily is handy.

Room-by-Room Focus:
It's All about Flow and Function

Not being a particularly handy family, we do not have a lot of tools, but we know how to use the ones we have. Some of the tools look similar—a straight-slot screwdriver versus a Philips head screwdriver—but each has a very specific purpose. Some tools have multiple purposes: a hammer can pound a nail into a board or pull one out.

Look at your home and the rooms that make it up with this same perspective. Think of your house as one big toolbox. Each room, be it a heavily used room or not, has a purpose or multiple purposes. Each room should be set up to accomplish its purpose effectively and efficiently, while expressing your family's personality.

With common areas in the home comes shared responsibility and often multiple uses. These are often the trickiest areas of any house. But the good news is, if set up efficiently, they are the rooms that give back the most as far as allowing your family to function. Rooms with only one or two primary occupants do not have to be as versatile, but are equally important to the big picture when it comes to how a family functions. If the rest of the family is in the car ready to go to school and you have one child digging through their room looking for a library book, the whole family is still late!

Whenever you consider organizing a specific area of your house, keep in primary consideration your family's daily habits and schedules.

There's no point in organizing a closet to a state you consider perfect if it's going to be destroyed within a week. This is probably a clue that your perfect system doesn't work for the whole family. You want organize to a level of functionality. Aesthetics are nice, but are secondary to the realistic application of your organizing efforts. Approach the job with realistic expectations of both yourself and your family.

Don't overwhelm yourself or your family by trying to restructure your whole home at one time. As stated earlier, change is most effective when taken in small increments. Let each change take root before moving forward. Enjoy your small successes in your pursuit of making more time for what really matters.

KITCHEN: THE HEART OF THE HOME

There is no place in a house that more defines

the home than its kitchen. Kitchens seem to have a certain magnetic attraction. They attract people, clutter, and some of the toughest cleaning and organizing challenges in the house. As with so many things in life, what brings out the best in us also brings out the worst.

Have you ever planned a party, carefully arranging seating around the house so that it is comfortable and conducive to conversation? People always end up in the kitchen, no matter how messy it is—even if the food is not in there! I actually think this is a good thing. I want people to feel comfortable in my home, both physically and emotionally, and the kitchen can lend itself to both. I would rather have people congregate in the kitchen and feel at home than let my personal "agenda" supersede their comfort and enjoyment.

If we were all as versatile as our kitchens, think how much we would get done. Talk about multitasking! The same room that feeds you is generally command central for family communications. Command central is also the family tutoring center (a kitchen table is a natural for homework). The tutoring center becomes the game room on family night and the conference room during family meetings. The kitchen table is also the psychologist's couch where two friends can share a cup of coffee and a heart-to-heart talk.

What a room! Fortunately, there are plenty of ways to support your kitchen's varied roles as natural meeting place, communication center, and heart of the home. The following tips and ideas will help you keep the heart of your home clean, organized, well stocked, and ready for anything.

Flow and Function

Flow and Function

Bright Ideas for the Kitchen

Get Ready to Get Organized

We tell our kids not to push their food around on their plates to make it look like they have eaten something. Why is it we often take this exact approach to organizing? We move the entire not-so-small collection of margarine tubs that we are sure we will need some day (even though we only have half the lids) to another shelf to make room for the blender, which we are moving from the counter to make room to write a grocery list because there is no longer any clear space on the kitchen table. This situation is not conducive to the serenity and peace of mind you and your family deserve!

57 **Clean so you can organize.** Always start with a clean slate. When you have set aside a block of time

to organize in the kitchen, make sure you are starting with a clean kitchen, otherwise the tendency is for your organizing time to turn into a basic cleaning session.

58 **Clear the decks.** Remember that to get to the deeper levels of organization that will really make a difference in your life, the basic stuff on top needs to be done already.

59 **Remember why you're doing this and get ready to let things go.** When organizing requires getting rid of things, as it usually does, we need to objectively assess everything we touch and determine its current state of functionality (or lack thereof) and the degree to which it will enhance our life experience. You must have yourself in the mental state to take an objective look and let go as necessary. Who knew this could take such mental discipline!

60 Before you begin to organize, remove everything from your target area (which is, say, a cabinet or section of counter), placing each item in a neutral location that has absolutely zero chance of becoming a permanent home. This is the time to make the first purge and get rid of those items you know need to go, so that you do not have to touch them again. Have an appropriate depository nearby for quick disposal. After everything is out, wipe down and thoroughly clean the area.

Keep It Handy

Having completely cleared out your target area, you're on your way to a new level of ease in the kitchen. Next you are going to prioritize the items taken out and placed in the previously established neutral territory. As you organize your kitchen, try to store everything as close as possible to where it will be used. This may seem obvious, but how many of us really have this figured out? Aesthetics are nice—yes, the canister might really look good there—but functionality is *king* (or queen) in the kitchen.

61 **Evaluate how often you use each item.** Is this cabinet or counter the most logical place for it? If so, start putting things away one at a time, with the most frequently used items in front. If an item is something you do not use very often, consider putting it in the basement or a storage location where it will be accessible but not contribute to the clutter in a high-use zone.

62 I have all my baking things in the drawer under the mixer, next to the range. Pots and pans are also near the range. The silverware is in the drawer nearest to the table.

63 Use a tiered wire desk organizer to store your cookie sheets, cutting boards, and other flat pans. They will be easily accessible and more sanitary. In the event that they were put away damp, they will have adequate airflow to dry, plus you will be utilizing vertical space that is often overlooked in cabinets.

64 Are you right-handed or left-handed? I did not realize how much difference this could make until we built our new house. In our old house, the dishwasher was to the left of the sink. I am right handed and now find that the suggestion of the builder to put the dishwasher to the right of the sink has made life much easier. It just seems to flow better. You might not be able to move your dishwasher, but consider where you tend to stand in the kitchen for various activities, at the range, at the sink, and at the counter where you do your prep work, and place tools and appliances strategically to these locations.

Making Space

Storage space in the kitchen is at a premium. Precious counter space often gets bogged down with clutter, and drawers fill up fast—especially if they're used haphazardly.

Flow and Function

65 **Make more room in your towel drawer by rolling your kitchen towels instead of folding them.** You will fit more in and they are handy to grab when you are in hurry and have wet hands.

66 **Use your kitchen wall space to get things off the counter!** From magnetic knife holders to hanging spice racks, if you have wall space, there is a product that will make it work for you.

Label Your Storage Areas

Keeping things in bins and boxes on shelves is a good, clean, space-efficient way to store less-frequently used items. It does, however, make things more difficult to find if the boxes and shelves are not labeled.

67

Create zones for similar items: decorations, out of season items, kitchen overflow, etc. Label the shelf and the container. Then put things back where they belong after using them. If you are really ambitious, take a photo of what is inside and tape it to the outside of the container.

Out of the Box

I was just taking a break from writing and went for a drink in the kitchen. There were keys in my refrigerator! Kris, one of my family's many angels, had taken the kids out to lunch so that I could get some good uninterrupted work done. She left her keys on top of her leftover box from the restaurant so she wouldn't forget to take her food with her. What a great example of thinking outside the box and utilizing a technique in a new way that creates an effortless solution.

Flow and Function

Spicy Tricks

You know my rule about keeping everything close at hand. I keep my spices in a deep drawer to the left of my range along with my primary cookbook, measuring cups, and spoons. I love the location, but I hated looking down at the tops of containers that all looked alike.

68 **Using your label maker, make labels for the tops of spice jars or any container stored below eye level.** If a spice has a particularly long name you may want to consider an acronym.

69 If your eyes are not as good as they used to be (I know I have become more and more dependent on my glasses) and you have trouble making out those little names, just put the initial letter or two on the label, and make it plenty big. At least it will narrow your choices!

70 **On the topic of spices, use a permanent marker and write the date of purchase on the jar or can.** As spices get old, they lose more and more of their punch. Although most do not give an expiration date, I doubt if their manufacturers intended that they be handed down for generations!

71 **Pool your resources.** I recently made a recipe that required a small amount of a rare spice I had never heard of. I'm not sure if I even pronounced it correctly when asking for help from the grocery store clerk to find it, although she was polite and did not correct me! A small fortune later, I had a whole jar of a spice of which I only needed a

Flow and Function

quarter teaspoon. A couple of days later I was telling my friend how much I enjoyed her recipe, thanking her for the good lead and made a half-joking comment about the spice. She laughed and said that she had thought the exact same thing. The lesson here: before spending big bucks on a spice you will rarely use, check and see if you can share it with a friend.

Give It Up, Let It Go, Say Goodbye

Native Americans have a nifty expression to describe something that has outlived its usefulness (if it ever had any). They say that it no longer grows corn. If something no longer grows corn for you, it's time to toss it, sell it, or give it away. My modern day translation: if it does not make my life more prosperous or easier, it is out of here!

72 "It is better to give than to receive" is a wonderful lesson to learn and made all the sweeter when both parties benefit from the generous act. Giving up the food processor you have not used in five years to the friend who has decided to make her own baby food gives her the means to follow through on an ambitious personal commitment. You, on the other hand, will not have to dust that appliance one more time, nor will you have to shuffle it around to make room for the next appliance *du jour* that is sure to make you the gourmet cook you have always wanted to be.

Conquering the Tyranny of Tupperware

It's amazing the impact of that constantly burgeoning plastic ware. As bad as you feel when it comes tumbling down on your head when

Flow and Function

you open the cupboard door, that's how good you will feel when you deal with it at last.

73 **Go through all of your plastic containers,** purchased, inherited, and—where *do* these things come from? Match each one with a top, and sort those that have tops from those that do not. Keep only the number of storage containers you can realistically use at any given time for your family.

74 **To dispose of those containers you no longer need, check with your child's school**—often they will be able to put them to good use in the classroom or art room.

75 **I have actually gone to glass storage containers;** they are a little more financial commitment up front, but they do not stain, they are easy to reheat in, and you can actually see what is inside. I keep fewer containers, cutting down on clutter—and they remain in better condition even after long use.

76 **Purchase a small stock of disposable containers** to use when entertaining to send family and friends home with leftovers to be enjoyed later (and remember the fun time had).

Make Friends with Your Refrigerator

If the kitchen is the heart of the home, the refrigerator may be what keeps the kitchen pumping. (Actually, it may be a toss up between the refrigerator and the kitchen table.) Unfortunately, refrigerators can be trouble, inside and out. Inside, things spill or get lost in the back for longer than we care to admit; outside, layers of notes, schedules, photos, artwork, and coupons pile up so thickly that the poor refrigerator magnets can't handle the load!

Let's work inside out. As far as I am concerned, the worst part of grocery shopping is putting things away when I get home (okay, paying is no walk in the park either). The temptation is to get it done as quickly as possible, ignoring or simply moving around items that really should be tossed. Resist this!

77

Take the time to go through the refrigerator every time you go to the store to determine what is out of date—or worse, unidentifiable. If you keep up with it on a regular basis this won't take long.

78 **Do what the stores do: place the items with the shortest expiration dates near the front.** Move to the freezer items that are likely to expire before you can use them.

79 **Once a week, go through papers stuck to the outside of the refrigerator** and toss or file anything that doesn't need to be there. An underbed plastic storage container is a great place to store your child's artwork at the end of its refrigerator rotation.

80 **The inside of a cabinet door is another good place to keep schedules and notes.** What was an eyesore on the front of the refrigerator will now be out of sight, yet still easily accessible. There are many self-adhesive hooks and clips available that will hold your papers neatly without damaging the cabinet surface. I admit I was forced into using the cabinets when I discovered that magnets did not stick on my beautiful new stainless steel fridge (and if you have ever tried to get tape off a standard finish appliance, multiply that by one hundred and you will know how hard it is on stainless). I must say, I am enjoying having a clear refrigerator. It has really helped in keeping the kitchen clutter free!

Your Office in the Kitchen

A desk or worktable in the kitchen is incredibly useful. I see it time and time again when I go into someone's home—usually piled with papers and other miscellaneous clutter. It often becomes the family dumping place.

81 Clean off the top of the desk at least once a week to make sure only current information is at hand. Only leave things on the desk that require your attention in the next couple of days. File or toss the rest.

82 Use stacking bins or tiered file organizers with clearly visible labels so you can quickly file incoming papers.

83 If you do not have room for files, use color-coded binder clips to clip related papers together. Hang these on the wall or side of a cabinet to get them off the top of your desk.

84 Review your system with your family and enlist their help in keeping the area organized. If the system is easy and obvious enough, everyone can use it.

85

Has your desk ever been so cluttered that you had to go sit at the kitchen table to pay bills? Next, a slow migration of clutter takes over the table, and you find yourself writing checks on the kitchen counter. **If a work area cannot be used for its original purpose, it is time to invest some time and elbow grease.**

Clearing Out and Cleaning Up

Cabinets are the greatest enabler of our intrinsic desire to place things out of sight and of mind without having to go through the emotional separation that occurs when we get rid of things. The bad news is, when they get so cluttered that you can't find anything, it robs you of your valuable time, not to mention your peace, tranquility, and ability to get places on time.

86 **Why not pick one cabinet a week to clean out?** Set a block of time each week—Monday morning, Thursday afternoon, whatever works in your schedule—for cabinet cleaning: kitchen, bathroom, or laundry. Choose one randomly, choose the one that's bugging you the most, or choose the one where you happen to be at that moment! Whatever you do, do not make choosing the hardest part of the task. With fifty-two weeks in a year, you can make sure that every cabinet is done at least once a year.

87 **Remember to clean inside and out** and to avoid the temptation of playing the shelf game; that is, moving items from one cabinet to another to achieve immediate results. These results may bring false immediate gratification, but only delay the inevitable.

Don't Forget the Top

I love tall ceilings with cabinets that do not go all the way to the top, but this does create another area to address when spring-cleaning comes along. Just because you cannot see the dust and dirt, does not mean it is not there!

88 After you have taken everything down, and wiped up all the dust and grime, **put down a semi-current newspaper to make for an easier cleanup the next time.** Spring comes every year. If you cannot readily recall who was president at the printing of the newspaper on top of your cupboard, you have skipped this task for too long!

Under the Kitchen Sink

A couple of years ago, in our old house, we had new kitchen countertops installed. With the countertops removed, looking down into the space beneath what had been the kitchen sink was enlightening. How many cleaning products does one house really need?

Clean out under your kitchen sink. Yuck! This is a terrible job. Completely empty the area and wipe it down. Since there are so many containers with messy liquids that have a tendency to spill or leak, using shelf liner will make clean-up much easier and preserve your cabinet.

Combine half-used duplicate products. (Hey, it happens to everyone.)

91

Toss all the products you were suckered into purchasing that promised to change your life and that you are now hanging on to because you are too embarrassed to admit, even to yourself, that you fell for such an obvious gimmick! The ideal of a clean house can entice a woman to buy almost anything; we all have our weak moments.

Go with Multiple Use

Specialty cleaning products and tools have really gotten out of hand. There are so many choices and many of the items have such a limited scope of use that they may not get used more than once. I think it is time to get back to the basics! Find products and tools that have multiple uses—and that you know work.

92 **Baking soda** is a great example: you bake with it, it helps deodorize the refrigerator, cleans crayon marks off the wall, and, in a pinch, you can even brush your teeth with it.

93 **Denture cleaning tablets are another item with multiple applications:** use a denture cleaning tablet to clean small or narrow necked vases and containers. Fill the container with water, drop in the tablet, and let it work for a few minutes. Empty, rinse, and you're done! They also work great for cleaning toothbrushes.

Enjoying Life in Your Kitchen

Now that your kitchen is in the kind of shape it deserves to be in, here are a few tips for making the most of it.

94

When your kids are really small, they love to be just like you and work in the kitchen. Take advantage of this willingness and show them where things are stored in the kitchen, especially the lower level shelves and cabinets that are easily accessible to them. When you bring groceries home or are emptying the dishwasher, leave those things that little hands can put away on the counter and let them pitch in. If you do not mind the "toddler interior decorator look," you could take a photograph of what is in the cabinet and drawers and tape it on the outside as a reminder.

95

Mornings can be stressful with all the hustle and bustle required for everyone to get out the door on time. **Lessen your morning rush by setting the table for breakfast the night before.**

Pull out the toaster with the loaf of bread and jar of peanut butter next to it. Put the cereal bowls, spoons, and your kids' favorite cereal on the table. With breakfast this ready to serve, your kids will feel as though they are just one step away from breakfast in bed! (Who knows, maybe they'll reciprocate with the real thing.)

Flow and Function

96 I love the opportunity to merge form and function. **Find a decent-looking silverware/napkin caddy to use as a centerpiece on your kitchen table.** Setting the table will be a breeze with the silverware close at hand.

97 **Use another caddy in the refrigerator for condiments that usually get pulled out at the same time anyway;** ketchup, mustard, mayo, and relish. With one

hand (which is how most of us usually function anyway) you will be able to grab what you need to set the table. One time in and out of the refrigerator will also help it run more efficiently, saving energy and money.

The Family Cookbook

98 **Create a family recipe book.** Have each member choose several favorite main dishes, side dishes, snacks, and desserts. Compile them using a three-ring notebook, sorting recipes by family member and then again by type of dish, or whatever arrangement you like. Create shopping lists for each recipe as you go along.

99 When someone prepares one of the recipes, **take pictures of the gourmet cook at work and add it to your book.**

100

Use the family recipe book when planning special family celebrations or to help include the whole family in weekly menu planning.

101

Take it a step further and **scan the recipes and pictures so you can make copies of your cookbook to share with family and friends as gifts!** (Thanks to my brother and sister-in-law for this great idea—with seven kids, I think her cookbook could compete with Betty Crocker's.)

A Tip of the Coffee Mug

I am so frustrated with myself! I had made it my whole life without drinking coffee in the morning and now suddenly, I am sucked in! Sure, I went through a Diet Coke phase, and when tea first became "in," I gave that a shot,

Flow and Function

and currently I am resisting the energy drink thing! But whatever the cause, I am now one of the mass of American moms who drive their kids to school with one hand on the steering wheel and the other holding a travel mug. The morning waves have been replaced with a polite tip of the mug! It all seems so civilized.

102 I love to **get the coffeemaker ready to go the night before:** clean filter, four scoops of ground coffee, and a measure of water, and morning has just gotten that much easier. In the morning all I have to do is press the button! Of course, if I would take the time to actually read the instructions (luckily, because of my filing system, I know exactly where they are), I could set the timer to have hot coffee waiting for me when I wake up. Maybe next year. (Remember, incremental change!)

Special Attention for the Kitchen

Although the kitchen usually does not have a door at all, if it did, I am sure it would be a revolving door. We are usually so busy during our time there that we complete the task at hand and that's it. This focus, combined with our amazing ability to see things through rose-colored glasses, sets the stage for the buildup of many incomplete or half-done projects and tasks that end up contributing to our sense of distress.

Once a week, take a hard, truthful look around. The following jobs are things you may be overlooking or just in complete denial about. They are also things that feel really, really good to accomplish. If you determine that something needs to get done and you know you can't attend to it immediately, put it on your calendar for next weekend (or the weekend after that) and relax. Now it's in your

Flow and Function

schedule, and it will actually happen! Approach everything you do with a great sense of achievement (no matter how small or insignificant it seems), not with regret for not getting to it sooner. As Harry S. Truman said, "Never, never waste a minute on regret. It is a waste of time."

103 Clean out under your sink.

104 If you ever sit down and read your **refrigerator** manual (like any of us have time for that) you will learn that we are supposed to **vacuum the filters on the back periodically for the highest energy efficiency.** Do not hurt yourself: get help pulling the refrigerator out from the wall and thoroughly vacuum the coils in back. Now, doesn't that feel good?

105 **Wipe down your cabinets inside and out.** If you do not have time to finish them all at once, at least get started with one or two.

106 **Even if it seems to be flowing fine, put some drain cleaner with a baking soda chaser in the sink to prevent future buildups.** It will also help eliminate odors.

107 **Clean out and organize the junk drawer** (you know you have one—or maybe two).

108 **Organize and clean your pantry or other location where you store your canned goods.** If there is anything there that you know you will not be using, donate it! Check the expiration date, if provided.

109 **Wash your kitchen floor on your hands and knees.** It is the only way to really see the dirt. (Warning: you may not like what you see—and this new perspective on your kitchen may lead to more projects!)

110 **Sort through your storage containers.** Donate or discard containers with no lids or with unsightly stains.

111 **Put Jet Dry in your dishwasher.** It really does work! It only took me forty years to figure this out.

112 **Clean out the inside of your refrigerator.**

113 **Recycle excess grocery bags, paper, and plastic.** My local grocery store has started offering a three-cent discount for every paper bag (in good shape, of course) that you bring in to re-use.

114 **Sort your silverware drawer and clean out the crumbs** (hopefully not chunks) on the bottom.

Flow and Function

115

If you have a desk or worktable in the kitchen, clean it off and organize any bills and papers.

LAUNDRY: A NECESSARY EVIL

I have come to believe that there is a laundry gene. Not like the jeans you wear on your body, but the genes that make up the very fiber of your being. You are either born with this laundry gene or, as in my case, not. I doubt that any geneticists are looking for this specific bit of DNA, but anyone like myself with this laundry deficiency knows that it can significantly affect your life and the lives of anyone else unlucky enough to live in your house and be dependent on you for their clean clothes.

One day at our bus stop, I noticed that one of the little boys had fold marks on his shirt which was otherwise very crisp and like new.

Now that I think of it, it was rather rude of me, but I asked his Mom if he had gotten a new shirt. Unfazed by my apparent lapse of judgment, she replied, "No, I am just a really good folder." A really good folder? I was still mulling over this concept when I stopped by her house a couple of days later (lapse of judgment number two—unannounced). My timing was perfect! What was she doing? Folding clothes! And you know what? She *is* a good folder! Not only does she fold precisely, she takes no more time with each piece than I do. Thank you, Mom and Dad, for good skin, functional intelligence, and workable coordination. But, could we have eliminated the gray hair gene and replaced it with the folding gene?

I may never be a good folder or a great laundry person. I still sometimes throw a red sock in with the whites and tumble dry a shirt that clearly specifies "dry flat" or "dry clean only" on the tag. Nevertheless, I *am* good at making sure my family always has the clothes they need at the times they need to wear them, clean towels to dry off with, and socks to put on their feet (please don't ask me about the holes). My family is the first to laugh with me when an occasional laundry blunder occurs and the last to complain if something needs ironing because it sat in the dryer too long!

Our family is reasonably well-dressed and clean, and we are happy with our level of laundry competence. If you or someone else in your home has the laundry gene and glories in fragrant stacks of perfectly pressed and folded clothing, that's good, too. Just look to see what works and what could work better for your family, and use the following tips to make laundry less of a chore.

Bright Ideas for the Laundry

Effortless Sorting

Sorting dirty laundry can be one of the most thankless, but critical jobs within the home. Instead of doing it all at once, which makes the whole laundry process seem more intimidating, not to mention increasing the margin for error, set up the following system.

116 **Help your family succeed in the sorting process by making it very visual.** Put two laundry baskets in all the bedrooms and any other locations that tend to collect dirty clothes on the floor. There are plenty of attractive choices available.

117 **Put a colored basket and a white basket side by side at each location.** You will probably not even have to

explain it once, but it is better to clearly explain your expectations than be surprised later. Colors go in the—yes, you guessed it—colored basket and whites in the white. If in doubt, put it in the color. As laundry is collected and brought to the laundry room, the job is already halfway done!

118 **Make sure you still do a quick scan as you put things in the washer**—no one is perfect!

Know Your Limitations

Knowing my lack of laundry savvy, I will not even attempt to wash my more delicate items—they go straight to the dry cleaner.

119 **I keep a separate basket in my closet to hold those clothes that require expert care.** Once a few pieces

have collected, I put them in the car so that when I'm running errands and have a few extra minutes, I can drop them off at our local dry cleaner.

Don't Fall into the Lint Trap

Most of us are diligent about cleaning out the lint trap after each load we take from the dryer, but did you know that the cleaning products we use in the washer and dryer can collect on the mesh and build up a film that decreases airflow and thus the dryer's effectiveness? This can cost you money, both in your electricity bill and in repair costs.

120 Remove the screen from the lint trap and wash it with soapy water and a small brush **once or twice a year.** You may be shocked by what you see. Remember that even if you do not see much, you are still removing the thin film that can cause you big trouble.

121

Go a little deeper. With the screen still out, use a small attachment on your vacuum cleaner to remove excess lint and bits of paper from the cavity.

122

I know I could be better about looking through pockets before clothes go into the washer, but I cannot believe the amount of paper that goes through my wash—sometimes the kind with pictures of famous people like George Washington on it. Which leads me to a **house rule: whoever does the laundry gets to keep what they find!** (When I recently found forty bucks with my son looking over my shoulder, he even considered doing laundry—albeit only for a moment.)

Flow and Function

Just Say No to Dryer Sheets

Personally, I think that fabric softener sheets are expensive and annoying. They always seem to pop up where they are not wanted. There is nothing more aggravating than getting undressed at the end of a long day only to realize you have been walking around with a dryer sheet stuck to the inside of your sweater! All of that being said, I have to admit I still use them some of the time. The following idea is great for everyday use, or just in a pinch.

Flow and Function

123 **Purchase liquid fabric softener in bulk.** Put it in a spray bottle and spray it onto a clean rag, old sock, or washcloth, which you toss into the dryer with the rest of your clothes. You will achieve the same effect as the disposable dryer sheets with less expense and waste.

Curing the Crinkles

Despite my attempts to progress in the area of laundry, I do still have the occasional load of clothes that sat overnight in the dryer and now have a really cool and pervasive crinkle. (If only that look would become the popular trend.)

124 **Wet a clean washcloth or hand towel and tumble it in with the dry clothes for a touch up.** The added moisture will have the clothes crisp in no time.

Start Them Young

Kids enjoy helping with the laundry, especially if you give them the best training you can and the proper tools.

125 As your younger kids start helping with laundry, **prepackage detergent (if you use powder) into Ziploc baggies** to ensure that the proper amount is used.

126 **Work with your children at the beginning** and show them step-by-step what needs to be done.

127 **Start the kids folding less difficult items first,** such as towels and undergarments.

128 Teach the kids to identify which items should be pulled out and hung on hangers immediately and which ones can be folded.

Sock Saga

I have a sign in my kitchen that says, "Because I said so." Along that same line of logic comes, "Because that is the way it has always been done." Here's a great example of how taking a little trouble to establish a new procedure can make life a whole lot easier.

Up until recently, I avoided sorting socks as they came out of the dryer, instead tossing them into the "sock basket." The sock basket was the source of much frustration in our house. When you ran out of socks, you were faced with the task of weeding through the basket to find two socks that matched (closely enough that no one else would notice) or sitting down and spending the time to sort through the whole thing. This was the way it had been done in my house growing up. I saw no need to change.

My husband's family, on the other hand, sorted socks as they came out of the dryer—they even turned their socks right side out. Imagine! I eventually started with the on-the-spot sorting and progressed to the turning right side out (again, incremental change). After finally coming over to the other side, I have to admit, their way is much easier! Why did I fight it? Because, "that is the way it has always been done." Accepting things the way they are, whatever their current state, usually feels a lot easier than making a change. Maybe it is—in the short run. If we can just look at the big picture, we can see how even a minor adjustment in how we do things can make life easier in the long run.

"Change is not made without inconvenience, even from worse to better."
—Richard Hooker

Special Attention for the Laundry

The laundry room is supposed to be a "clean area." Unfortunately, we often clean our clothes in a less than sparkling environment. Take a few moments a couple of times a year (perhaps even more often) to accomplish these easy tasks that will make laundry more enjoyable (okay, maybe that's the wrong word).

129 **Toss or recycle as a dust rag any sock that has not had a match** in longer than you would like to admit.

130 Get help moving **your washer and dryer, and clean under-neath and behind.**

131 Clean the top and sides of the washer and dryer thoroughly.

132 Vacuum the dryer's lint screen and basket.

133 Organize your laundry supplies; if you could use a new laundry basket or drying rack, add it to your shopping list.

134 Keep a jar for stray change in the laundry room. Cash it in periodically for a little treat.

135

Don't be intimidated! Discard damaged or excess hangers.

BEDROOMS: A PLACE FOR PEACE AND QUIET

Most other areas of the house are what we consider common areas that need to function and flow in a way that meets the needs of the entire family. Bedrooms are really the place where each family member can express their own style and personality. For husbands and wives, there may need to be some more compromise. Although you want this space to be reflective of its inhabitants, it should still be functional.

Bright Ideas for Kids' Bedrooms

If we as parents are Kings and Queens of the Castle, our children are Prince and Princess of the Palace—that is, their own rooms. Much of the house, as it should be, is decorated and arranged according to how grown-ups see it and use it. Children's rooms can be an area of some debate. We want our kids to express themselves in the decoration of their rooms and keep their rooms reasonably picked up. The problem is…we want them to do it according to our standards. This is an age-old debate that clearly has some middle ground.

Décor (or Lack Thereof)

When we moved into our new home, Kyle was in charge of putting things away in his own room. He took great pride and put much effort into placing his trophies, organizing his Game Boy games, cords, and all those other things that I am not really sure what they do. And he did a great job! He effectively created an organizing system that must have a secret code that only he knows! Brilliant, really. I cannot find anything, but he knows where everything is—or is not. Come to think of it, he probably has the same experience when he goes into my office looking for something.

Lesson learned—just because it is not done my way, does not mean it is not done! If the system works for them and keeps their room reasonably picked up, let it go. (Someone please keep reminding me of this revelation.) I don't think I am alone in saying that giving up control is one of the most difficult things about being a parent as our children grow! A great place to start is with your children's rooms. Besides, you can always close the door.

Self-Expression

Children want you to show and feel a full

appreciation for every piece of artwork they make. Displaying their masterpieces can be a challenge. You want them to be visible, yet be able to change them out quickly as new works are finished.

136 **Use string and clothespins to create a custom border in your child's room.** Secure the string with small nails at regular intervals around the room. Use the clothespins to hang artwork, photos, and other important papers. They will be easy to change out and add great personality to the room.

137 **If your house has maxed out its limits for children's art, consider framing one of the more distinctive pieces and making a gift of it to grandma**

or grandpa. If the masterpiece is oversized, take a photo of it to frame, or have the graphic made into note cards! What a treat it would be for family and friends to receive a handwritten note on a card with such personal significance.

138 Use an inexpensive plastic tackle box to store all your young children's art supplies. Consolidating all their materials into an easily transportable container will help keep things together and in working order. (Is it just me, or are crayons more fragile than they used to be?) Separate the different items into small baggies to help keep the box organized. Before the box is put away, make a quick check to make sure things were put away properly. You and you children will appreciate this extra step when the box is pulled out for its next use.

On Their Level

Take a tour of your child's room from their perspective. Get down on your hands and knees if your children are very small, or just on your knees if they are a little bigger. What do you see? Do you see toys and pictures, or do you see the legs of the bed, dresser, and nightstand?

139 **Put the things your child uses at their level**—mirrors, pictures, and mostly importantly, toys. I have seen beautiful rooms for small children that have all the toys displayed on shelves well beyond the child's reach. Put toys in easily accessible containers so that your child can take them out and—more importantly—put them back by themselves. Under the bed is a great place to store toys if you use containers and keep the area organized.

140

Lower the pictures on the walls to their eye level. Can you imagine walking into your kitchen one morning to find that your counter tops had been raised to forty-six inches instead of the standard thirty-six inches? You'd need a step stool to make your coffee. Just as you would feel like a fish out of water, it is easy for kids to feel the same way in their own rooms.

141

Let's face it, even adults have a difficult time keeping their closets in order, and most of us can reach the hanging bar! **Use an adjustable drop-down closet rod to help bring clothes down to your child's level.** Use simple hangers that are size appropriate for your child's clothes to make it easier for them. Use the upper area of the closet to store out-of-season clothes.

Don't Fight It

Whenever possible, the path of least resistance can make everyone's life easier!

142 If your children don't exactly have the knack of hanging their clothes in the closet, install hooks on the back wall of the closet or on an accessible wall to provide them an easy alternative to throwing their clothes on the floor. Hangers appear to be a simple tool, but even as parents we sometimes get frustrated with them: the shirt that keeps slipping off, or not being able to find a pants hanger when you need one, or getting the silly things tangled up when you're in a hurry. That's when chairs, benches, and exercise equipment become dumping places for us! Are we that much different than our children? Hooks will

give the kids an easy way out and achieve your goal of keeping clothes off the floor.

Where to Put It?

I love that old adage, "A place for everything and everything in its place."

143

Out of Sight. Use low profile, under-the-bed storage containers to store old school papers that have left the refrigerator circuit, or for out-of-season clothing. This accomplishes two purposes; it provides extra storage and also takes up space that otherwise would be a catchall or hiding place when it comes time to clean. Some of the storage containers even have wheels, which make it easy for small children to pull out and put back.

144 **You're Never Too Young to Categorize.** Start your children very young learning how to sort and categorize their own possessions. Make sure to establish categories that are appropriate for their age and skill level. When kids are very young, toys might be the only category. All their toys go into one big box or basket. The next step would be three boxes or bins separating large, medium, and small toys. Finally, you can introduce basic categories, moving out of the box method. Work with them to sort their possessions into basic categories such as stuffed animals, books, electronics, trading cards, etc. Work together to assign a home for each grouping. Just as we tend to create zones in our areas of the house, the same strategy works great in kids' rooms. Make sure to include your child throughout

Flow and Function

the process. You will be there to help with large cleanups, but the goal is to create an environment that they find easy to maintain.

145 **Money-Saving Tip.** Find a couple of large, sturdy cardboard boxes to use as temporary toy boxes (check with local stores that will give you their shipping cartons). Have your child help you cover the boxes in wrapping paper, or let them really show their creativity and paint or draw on them! If they get beat up or start falling apart, make replacing them a rainy day activity. Decorate the boxes to celebrate the holidays!

Location, Location

Here's a great opportunity to be creative and figure out what really works for your kids.

146

Use low shelves and drawers to store the most frequently used items. Who ever said that underwear needs to go in the top drawers? No one that I know of, yet where do we always put it? Shake things up. Put the clothes your kids wear the most on the bottom and move the less frequently used or seasonal stuff up top! Your kids will be able to get out and replace their clothes with greater ease.

147

In real estate, the catch phrase is "location, location, location." In our kids' rooms it should be "storage, storage, storage." You can never have enough. **Make sure you have plenty of drawers, hangers, hooks, baskets, and bins for everything in the room.** (If their room is looking more like a storage unit than a bedroom, it is time to start saying goodbye to some things!)

Flow and Function

In the Zone

I was first introduced to the idea of zones when my children were young and attended daycare. (With all those kids and more toys than Santa could carry in his sleigh, they have to be experts.) Although I had never called it "zones," I had been organizing my space in this way for years.

148 **What are your child's favorite activities?** Choose three or four and assign each to a corner of the room as a zone if you have room, or only two or three if space is tight. Arrange furniture and toys to make these areas function for that activity. Put like activities in the same general location. For example, in my daughter's play area, we have a very diverse doll zone. Barbie, an American Girl, Hopscotch Girls, and babies all share the same address.

Do It Together

Help your children make an investment in their own space by being active in creating an environment that is both comfortable and functional for their needs. This is one of the hardest for me. I often start out listening to their ideas, but my tendency is to try a little too hard to interject my ideas. I can tell when I start down this path, because my son stops coming up with his own creative ideas and instead just asks me what I think he should do. It breaks my heart when I do this, but at least when I am aware of it, I can catch myself and turn the situation around.

149 **Always try to end a project on a positive note, with your child feeling good about what he or she has suggested or done.** Even if things do not turn out exactly the way you would have done it, if your child takes ownership in their room and they feel that you supported them, they will work harder to keep it organized.

150 **Cleaning out toys can be an emotional task for all parties involved!** Have your children help you place every toy into one of four piles; keep, donate, toss, or needs repair. Evaluate everything and determine what works and what does not, what is missing pieces, and what can be replaced. It is a good idea to have an extra stash of batteries of all sizes available for this task. You can't tell if something works with dead batteries, and you do not want to keep it or donate it if it is broken!

151

Although sorting toys with the kids involved can add some stress, it is a good lesson for them to carry forward as adults—YOU CAN'T KEEP EVERYTHING! One thing my kids have enjoyed, which helps end the job on a positive note, is to **allow them to take back one toy from the "donate" or "toss" pile when the job is finished.**

Label, Label, Label!

Clear storage containers are great because you can see what is in them, but they also can make an organized area look cluttered if the contents are just thrown in. The trade off, if you choose to use baskets or solid containers, is you cannot see what is in them, but once on the shelf you will have a neater look.

Flow and Function

152

Whichever storage method you prefer, it is important to label the contents of each container to help in the process of both finding things and putting things away. Make labels large enough so that they are easy to read, and affix them securely so that they will not fall off.

153

For young children who are non-readers, draw a picture—or better yet—take a picture of what is inside and adhere it to the outside of the box.

A Picture Is Worth a Thousand Words!

I am sure I am not the only mom who has a different opinion than her child on what clean means and, more importantly, what it looks like. "Clean your room" is a very vague comment to a ten-year-old!

154 **Help your child clean their room to a reasonable standard—** probably somewhere between what you consider clean and what they consider clean—and take a photo of the finished product. Put the picture in a drawer or some place where it will be accessible. When you ask your child to clean their room, they can refer back to the picture before they declare the job done. If they have hurried through, hopefully they will realize it by seeing what the room *should* look like, and save you from having to deliver the bad news.

Flow and Function

Daily Routine

The great thing about a daily routine is that it becomes habit, so neither you nor the kids have to keep reinventing the wheel.

155

Help your kids establish a simple checklist of things they need to get done every day. Lovingly, hold them accountable to this list. Help them to establish the routine and make it habit by completing the items in the *same* order every day until they become second nature. Get up, brush your teeth, make your bed, feed the dog, eat breakfast. Or, get up, eat breakfast, brush your teeth, make your bed, feed the dog. The order should be one that fits your child's personality and how they react to mornings.

156

Surprise your kids by offering to make their beds for them in the morning! Now, this is only a meaningful gesture if you do not regularly make it and/or no one makes it! One nice thing about establishing a daily routine that

Flow and Function

includes the accomplishment of basic regular tasks is that it offers you the opportunity to do something nice for them with very little effort. When I offer to make my son's bed, you would think from his level of appreciation that I had saved him from a half hour job!

Make a Game of It

Make cleaning up fun for your kids and you'll be rewarded by their easy cooperation.

157 One of my daughter's favorite shows has a segment called **the ten-second tidy.** Unless your children can move in a fast-forward speed, you may need to extend the time slightly. Set the timer for two or three minutes. Challenge your kids to see how many things they can pick up and put away in an orderly

fashion. Picking up and simply moving something from one location to another does not count. Do not start the timer until they start the work. If they take a break to complain, stop the timer until they resume their work. Be sure to offer a small reward and lots of encouragement for a job well done!

158

A little competition never hurt anyone, either. See who can pick up the most and offer a small reward. Make sure the competition is on a level playing field—if you have a younger child, give them a head start.

Tips for Teens

As your kids get older and more mature, make sure you give them a little more latitude in developing their own personality and style (as long as that style is not modern day pigpen). Help them to understand that you are asking them to keep their room at a functional level for their own benefit, not just to make their lives miserable or fulfill some fantasy you have of the perfect house. They will be happier if they are able to find stuff and keep their possessions from being ruined by neglect and disorder.

159 **If room-tidying seems to be a daily struggle, consider instituting the once-a-week rule.** Once a week (let your child pick the day) their rooms need to be clean, to a mutually agreed upon, predetermined level of organization. After all, what can get lost in a week? (Don't answer that.)

Bright Ideas for the Master Bedroom

The master bedroom is such an important room of the house; it is where the grown-ups (who are supposed to be setting the tone and running the show) start and end each day. It is a place to rest and rejuvenate. It is where relationships are strengthened and preserved. It is an adult space that no parent should feel bad about claiming as their own.

Unfortunately, perhaps because it is not on public display, the master bedroom tends to be one of the last rooms in the house to get decorating attention, updating, or even deep cleaning. How much attention have you given this special space since you bought your marital bed? (Please tell me you bought a marital bed—perhaps one of those waterbeds we dreamed of once upon a time.) Here are some tips and ideas to give your master bedroom the respect it deserves.

Keys to Compromise

Nowhere is the blending of two personalities more important than in the master bedroom. You have two genders that need to feel equally safe, comfortable, and relaxed in a setting that is still functional. Flowers or no flowers? Quilt or comforter? Fan or no fan? TV or no TV? Big, fluffy pillows or flat, hard pillows?

Flow and Function

160 You and your spouse, or significant other, should **make a list of the attributes of your ideal bedroom.** First do this independently from one another.

161 It's probably best to agree to be realistic and within your current budget and resources. Unless, of course, you both want to make "dream lists" with the understanding that some things may need to be worked toward.

162 **Get together and go through your lists.** Concentrate first on those items that you have in common. If these are missing, it should be easy to agree to include them in your bedroom life together.

163 **Next, identify those things where differences can be accommodated with ease.** I like big fluffy pillows, Dave likes flat hard pillows—so we have two of each. I can make the bed and still have it be symmetrical; flat pillows on the bottom with the fluffy pillows stacked on top—important to me, not so much to Dave!

164

Lastly, look at the true differences, approaching them with **a willingness to compromise.** After fourteen years of marriage, I have adjusted to having the fan running all night, 365 nights a year, and dare I say have become dependent on the soothing noise.

Relish Your Sleep

Keep in mind that the primary purpose of your bedroom (now, now, besides *that*) is *sleep*. As I get older, sleep becomes more and more important to me. I love this sleep cycle of life. When we were small infants, we slept all the time without coaxing or pressuring, and with absolutely no remorse. As toddlers, we fought tooth and nail *not* to sleep! As teenagers we fought tooth and nail *to* sleep! As parents, we want and need to sleep, but often feel guilty

Flow and Function

and pulled by too many other things. As grandparents (from my personal observation), we will go back to sleeping without coaxing or pressuring, and with absolutely no remorse!

Because you are reading this book, I suspect you are in the guilt phase along with me. We go-go-go and then, when we finally stop, we expect our bodies to fall asleep, just like that.

I don't know about you, but there are days when my body does not get the memo! We need all the help we can get, and setting up your bedroom to accommodate sleep will trigger the response when you are ready.

165

Create a peaceful atmosphere in your room that is conducive to your sleeping patterns. Experts agree that the room should be quiet, dark, and comfortable. To accomplish this, we put up the type of blinds that lay flat to keep out more light. If your blinds don't block enough light, try heavy drapes, or a combination of drapes and blinds.

166 Discuss with your partner what sort of background noise, if any, you would both find conducive to sleep. There are many catalogs and websites with devices for generating soothing, sleep-friendly sounds, such as gentle waves on the shore.

Protect Your Peace

Space in most houses is limited, and the master bedroom is often the quietest place in the house during the day. Because of this, you may be using the space for other purposes that deter from its peacefulness. You do not have adequate, peaceful darkness at night with the light of your computer monitor glowing at you, or a fax machine going off in the middle of the night. Although a treadmill or stair climber is great for hanging clothes on, you are doing yourself a disservice if your last thought of the day is self-defeat for not using it, or how soon you can wake up and jump back on that treadmill!

167 **Whenever possible remove these distractions from your bedroom.** If that's not a realistic option for you, try to screen off the office/exercise area with an inexpensive room screen. They make great ones that are actually picture frames (what better way to disguise a distraction than with comforting family photos), but they also are available in many beautiful styles.

Flow and Function

168 If you must have an office in your room, why not put to good use the one universality we are all good at—out of sight, out of mind! **Consider an all-in-one cabinet that you can close up at night to put the distraction out of sight.**

Dare We Say—Privacy?

If you have young children in your home, you may have forgotten the meaning of the word "privacy." If this is so, steal privacy where you can, and know that one day you may miss the lack thereof.

169 **As your kids get older, set rules of privacy for bedrooms and common bathrooms.** Do not do this in an intimidating way, but in a way that is respectful and loving. Through this process, we are teaching our children how to define their areas of privacy respectfully. As always, be sure to set rules and guidelines that work for your family, taking into consideration their personalities and maturity level.

Special Attention for the Bedroom

We want our personal space to be clean and inviting. After all, it may be the only place in the house where we can get away from it all. Take time once a month to give some extra special attention to this important space.

170 Vacuum under the bed.

171 Clean and organize the closet.

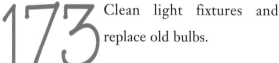
Go through accessories and donate those that are (or should be) out of style!

Clean light fixtures and replace old bulbs.

Clean out nightstand drawers.

Wash (or otherwise clean) the window treatments.

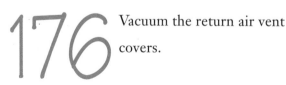
Vacuum the return air vent covers.

177 Dust the ceiling fan. Hanging dust bunnies are not an upgrade option.

178 Dust the baseboards and the top of the doorframes.

179 **Check for cobwebs in the corners of the room** and remove with a feather duster or vacuum attachment.

BATHROOMS: THE REAL UTILITY ROOM

When we refer to the utility room in a house, we usually think of the laundry room or even that scary, dark, unfinished area in the back of the basement that houses the organs of the house: furnace, hot water heater, etc. Webster defines utility as, "serving primarily for utility [that is, something useful or designed for use] rather than beauty." Boy, does that describe the bathrooms in my house. Most of us approach the bathroom with the "do what you've got to do and get out" attitude. Here are some tips to help you keep things in order, eliminate clutter, and cleverly disguise everyday items.

Bright Ideas for the Bathroom

Taking the time to organize your bathroom will not only make it more pleasant and give you additional space, it will also help you get in and out more quickly.

180 **Install a flip-out caddy under the bathroom sink,** the kind usually used under the kitchen sink for sponges and scrubbies. It makes a great place for toothbrush and toothpaste, especially for the little people.

181 **If you currently have a flat mirror on the wall, consider trading it for a medicine storage cabinet.** There are some great looking products available that can conceal toiletries and medicines behind closed doors, yet keep them close at hand.

182 **Over-the-door shoe organizers can be a great way to organize toiletries,** especially if the bathroom is shared by more than one person. Assign each person a pocket or two. Everything they need will be easy to access, yet hidden from sight. There are similar mesh pocket shower organizers for shower supplies.

183 **Colorful towels can become a functional accessory when rolled** and placed strategically in a big basket on the counter or a shelf by the tub. The towels will be close at hand when you need them, and you will be saving space in your linen closet!

184 **Keep disposable cleaning wipes in all the bathrooms in your house.** Bathrooms clearly need the most maintenance when it comes to cleaning! With a quick fix close at hand, you will be more likely to clean up the little messes before they become a major cleaning job. Kids aren't the only culprits when it comes to sloppiness in the bathroom. Am I the only grown-up still who cannot brush her teeth without getting toothpaste splatters on the mirror? With a quick swipe of a window wipe, the evidence is gone.

185 Hooks on the bathroom wall are great for hanging towels to dry, pajamas, or even clothes in preparation for the next morning.

186 Use a basket or decorative box to hold a roll or two of backup toilet tissue. The true utilitarian will throw caution to the wind, foregoing the basket or box, and hang an over-the-tank tissue holder. Not necessarily pretty, but without a doubt useful!

187 Put wasted space to good use. Use an over-the-toilet shelving unit to store extra towels.

188 **Get things out of the bathroom altogether.** Give each of your kids a basket or caddy for their personal items. They can keep it in their bedrooms and bring it in as needed. This also makes it easier to use another bathroom if necessary.

189 Bathroom vanity cabinets have storage space, but most of it is not easily accessible. **Use a pull-out tray on the bottom to keep things in the back within reach.** Using a freestanding shelf over that will give you two tiers of storage.

Special Attention for the Bathroom

I think even the most cleaning impaired among us don't let *basic* bathroom cleaning go for too long. The following tasks are aimed toward further enhancing your family's health and well-being.

190 Clean out under the sink.

191 Organize and clean cabinet drawers.

192 Give your medicine cabinet a check up. Flush any medications that have passed their expiration dates. Make sure you have an ample supply of over-the-counter medicines for basic needs.

193 Check your first aid kit and make sure it is fully stocked.

194 Use spray cleaner and a brush to clean your showerhead.

195 **Clean the light fixtures.** If you have an exposed bulb fixture, dust the bulb. (Note: Make sure the bulb is not hot.)

196 Check hair dryers, curling irons, electric razors, and other appliances for frayed or damaged cords.

ENTRYWAYS: WELCOME HOME

Your home's entry, be it the front door or the door from the garage, sets the tone for your family's return home after a long hard day at work or school. Nothing says welcome home more than an organized area that has a place for everything.

There are two types of visitors that come to your home: front door guests and back door friends. Just as people develop first impressions within the first three seconds of meeting someone, people make the same judgment regarding your home. It is my goal to make the front door guest feel welcome and comfortable enough to exit by the back door knowing that they can come back anytime.

Bright Ideas for Entryways

Entryways, especially the one the family uses most frequently, seem to be the common dumping ground in every home: backpacks, shoes, papers, baseball gloves, boots, briefcases, mail, and everything else your family gets their hands on throughout the day. Do you find yourself always justifying to your friends why they have to step over three pairs of shoes, two skateboards, and the dog's favorite squeaky toy to enter the house? Is your husband tired of never having a place to set down his briefcase when he comes in? Do even the kids complain that they can never find a matching pair of mittens in the jumble by the door?

The entries to your home should be as organized, comfortable, and inviting as the rest of it. That said, often there is very little space to work with. When faced with an organizing problem, I like to challenge myself to think "outside the box." I love that saying. Come to think of it, why would we ever want to be *in* the box? I want to show my kids how to be creative and solve problems with new solutions whenever possible.

The Locker Solution

Take a cue from those establishments that manage to handle thousands of young people every day, backpacks, boots, and books included: schools. My son, Kyle, is starting middle school in the fall. The two things he is most excited about are the cafeteria and the lockers. He has already made sure that locker accessories are a part of our back-to-school shopping list and budget!

197 In a culture where retro is in, many catalogs offer metal school-type lockers. Real lockers are great and can hide a multitude of sins. Unfortunately, many of them come with a

price tag that is definitely not retro! **Fortunately, there are many common household items that can be used to achieve the same basic results.**

The Basket Solution

If lockers are not in your budget or if you do not have the space, use laundry baskets for each member of your family to create an organized dumping zone. Mornings are hectic enough without hunting for the all-elusive mitten. Using the basket system, you will increase your chances of leaving the house without an annoying hunt for personal possessions.

198 **It's key for each person to have their own basket.** Kids might enjoy decorating theirs. When they enter the house, their possessions go there—shoes, mittens, and all.

199 The baskets can be stored under a bench, at the bottom of a closet, or even outside the door in the garage.

200 Keep a basket or shopping bag by the door as an errand basket. As you think of things you will need for running errands—videos and library books to return, dry cleaning to drop off, etc.—place them in the bag. Grab the bag or basket each morning as you head out. You will be prepared when you have a little extra time during the day.

The No-Space Solution

201 No room for lockers or laundry baskets? Hang an over-the-door shoe organizer on the back of the door. Keep shoes, mittens, hats, keys, and any other small items that tend to get lost and or misplaced. They will be ready and waiting when you are ready to leave!

202 If your climate and space provide, start the organizing outside in the garage.

And We're Off...

We all can use help getting out the door in the morning. Look for helpful objects that are both beautiful and utilitarian.

203 Use a decorative keyhook on the wall as a home for your key ring. These are available in styles to suit any decor—craft fairs are a great place to seek them out.

204 **An entryway is a natural place for a wall mirror,** creating openness as well as allowing you to check your appearance on your way out. Again, arts and crafts stores and fairs are a good source—buying a small mirror can be an affordable way to patronize an artisan whose work you admire.

Welcome Home

205 **Make sure you have a way to handle wet outer garments.** Put up pegs or a coat tree to accommodate them.

206 **Don't forget the doormat.** You might want to have a rugged one outside the door for scraping off the worst of the mud, and another inside to finish the job. An old-fashioned boot scraper is also a very practical device.

Special Attention for Entryways

You'll want to spend a few minutes each weekend organizing entryway areas so baskets or lockers don't overflow.

 **207** Gather the shoes that seem to collect in this area and put them back where they belong.

208 Put mittens without a mate into a specially designated basket, so when a spare turns up, you'll know where to look for its match. (Works for socks, too.)

209 Floors in this area get the most wear—sweep or vacuum here twice as often.

210 Hose off the doormats every couple of weeks—more often in messy weather.

Top to Bottom:
How to Get Your Whole Life Running Smoothly

Making time for what really matters begins with the small things in life. You want to take all those little variables and tasks that tend to stay on your mind and steal your time and energy, and get them handled. This chapter contains ideas for streamlining the activities in the various areas of your life and creating structures that can accommodate a few bumps along the way.

GETTING STUFF DONE: HANDLE IT ALL WITH EASE

Multitasking

I speak of multitasking often and think it is one of the greatest ways to significantly increase your productivity. There are so many things around the house that can be done simultaneously without compromising one another. Oftentimes they will even complement one another. Here are a few specific ideas for incorporating the concept of multitasking into your daily life. With technological advancements, it is easier than ever. Once you get the hang of it, you'll find it comes naturally.

211 **Get a phone with a headset.** Return calls as you fold clothes or do the dishes.

212 If you have a cell phone plan with unlimited minutes, use the commute time between school, practices, and doctor appointments to return calls. I try to make calls only on the leg of the trip that includes no kids. I love being in the car with my kids—they are captive and have to listen to me. On a good day, they will even talk!

213 Clean out your car while you are waiting for your kids after practice.

214 Fill even the smallest gaps of time with a productive activity. Waiting for the toaster—wipe down a counter. Boiling water—empty the dishwasher.

What? Nothing to Do?

Something weird happens when we find ourselves with some unscheduled free time—our minds go to mush! Projects, what projects? Before you know it, the moment or hour has passed and nothing got done. That's not necessarily a bad thing, but if you *are* motivated to get something done, it helps to be prepared.

215 **Start a wish list of those tasks and projects** you would like to get done sometime in the future, but with no specific deadline. Break them down into manageable tasks.

216 **Keep your wish list someplace where you can refer to it** on those rare days when the planets align, no kids are sick, the phone does

Running Smoothly

not ring, and you find yourself in an unfamiliar state of leisure! You can check your list, chose a task, and knock it off, 1-2-3.

The Nuts and Bolts List

Some things absolutely need to be done to keep your family functioning. When a wish list day seems a hundred miles away and you are having one of those days when nothing goes right and you are hanging on for dear life, fall back on this list.

217

Create a list of things around the house that are the nuts and bolts. This is very personal to *your* family and doesn't have to resemble anyone else's idea of what's important.

218

When you're feeling over-whelmed, eliminate every-thing else from your to-do list, and stick to the basics. Allow yourself the satisfaction of knowing that you're accomplishing the things that are most important to your family—that's something to be proud of!

Things to Do: Have Fun

Most of us are very professional about our to-do lists. We write down what we have to do and cross it off when the task is done. Not especially exciting (even if you're into this type of thing). We are the first to praise and reward our children for a job well done, but the last to acknowledge ourselves. When was the last time you put something fun on your to-do list?

219

List taking a bubble bath or sitting and watching the sunset with your favorite book, anything that gives you a lift. It's also a good idea to schedule a specific time.

220

Another advantage to writing a reward for yourself on your to-do list is that as you cross off your other tasks, you can see you are one step closer to your reward.

Does It Work for You or Against You?

Once a habit is formed, good, bad, or indifferent, it is hard to break. Several years ago, I moved the location of the garbage can in the kitchen from under the sink to another cabinet. I cannot begin to tell you how many times I still went under the sink to throw something away.

221

Take a look at your habits, good and bad. Is what you consider to be a good habit still productive, or have you maintained it just because that's how you have always done it? What are your bad habits? How could you change it into a good habit? The longer a habit persists, the harder it is to change.

The "P" Word

Procrastination really should be a four-letter word! Did you ever throw your hands up in the air and admit you are a procrastinator, as if it is something you can't change? What if it doesn't have to be that way? We *all* are capable of change—at any age. Here are some strategies to consider.

222 **Jump-start your day by accomplishing something right away**—before relaxing with your cup of coffee! Save your reward time for later when you can savor your accomplishments. Avoid the trap of rewarding yourself up front because you just *know* you're going to have such a busy day.

223 We all get caught in the trap of over-committing. **Take a look at what you are saying *yes* to.** Are they things that are important to you and your family, or did you feel pressured into making the commitment? If you say yes to something and then resent the time it takes to follow through, it probably is something you should not have agreed to in the first place.

224 If you get sweaty palms when you know you should say no, begin by saying a half no: "I really can't today, but I may be able to sometime in the future." It is a good way to get out of a pressure situation. Work yourself up to a definitive NO. Remember you are trying to retrain yourself; it is going to take time.

Done before You Know It

Purposely set roadblocks for yourself that force you to get things done. A job actually can seem easier if you've catapulted yourself halfway into it.

225 Move all the chairs and rugs from the floor in the morning in preparation for washing it. With little more effort than it requires to move everything back (which would be accepting defeat), you can wash the floors.

226 **Separate your dirty clothes in piles in the middle of the floor.** You will either have to get the laundry done that day, or pick them up to put back into the baskets.

The Ten-Minute Task

227 **Keep a list of tasks you can complete in ten minutes or less.** Any time you find yourself with a little time, you can accomplish one of these no-brainers.

228 **The power of multiples can turn your ten-minute tasks into forty minutes' worth**

of accomplishment if you get your family on board. Challenge everybody available to see how much you can get done in a mere ten minutes.

Possible Pitfall

229 **Be careful about concentrating only on the smallest tasks**—the tendency will be to reward yourself before the bulk of the work is done. You may feel like you're getting a ton of work done, but there is no end to the small stuff, and you may never get to the big stuff! Sometimes you have to tackle the large, more involved tasks first. Often you can work in the smaller tasks as you go along.

Projects

One of the greatest challenges to getting things done around the house is a lack of specific hard deadlines, especially for the bigger projects. When you work outside the home there are deadlines that, if missed, may negatively affect your paycheck. Hmm...I can't remember getting a paycheck for cleaning out the basement or organizing the closets. Several of our friends had kids graduating from high school last spring. It was amazing to watch projects they had been putting off for years get done in a weekend with all hands on deck. The difference was that they now had a deadline.

230 **Create deadlines for even the smallest of projects.** If you want to clean out your basement, schedule a truck to come pick up the things you are discarding before you even start the job. Need to clean out the refrigerator? Make a commitment to yourself not to

go to the grocery store again until it is done. (If you stick with this long enough, your family will probably do it for you!)

231 How many times have you put off or even given up completely on a project that seemed too big? Getting started is often the hardest part of an intimidating project. **If a project seems too big, break it down into smaller tasks.** Take one task at a time, but make sure you complete them in a timely way so that you do not lose sight of the larger goal.

232 If you are totally overwhelmed by what you see when you look around your house, call in help. There are professional organizers who are well worth the money, but I like the idea of buddying up with a friend to organize each other's houses. Take on your house one week and hers the next. Share resources and ideas for tackling the difficult areas. Do something fun together to reward yourselves when you are done.

Sample Action Plan

For more involved tasks, you may want to write up a short action plan. Here's a sample—a real plan I used to get basement clutter under control after we moved. Until I made up this plan, I felt overwhelmed and unhappy every time I looked at (or even thought about) the basement and its chaos. Just jotting down this plan made me feel better—I could see in black and white that there were a finite number of very doable steps to get me where I wanted to go. Breaking down a big project this way also makes it easy to ask for help: you can even make a wall chart with big boxes for you or other family members to check off when a mini-step is completed. Next thing you know, you'll have the thing done, and you can get to the good part—the reward!

Task: Organize Basement

Items Needed to Complete Task:

1. Shelving
2. Label maker
3. Tape
4. Clear plastic containers—large, medium, and small
5. Old shoe boxes
6. Newspaper for packaging
7. Garbage bags

Time Estimate Required to Complete Task: 7 *hours*

Running Smoothly

Steps to Complete:

1. Sort—keep, garbage, donate, or sell

2. Categorize

3. Repackage

4. Label

5. Assemble shelves

6. Organize items on shelves

7. Label shelves—so *everyone* know where to put things back

8. Dispose of garbage items

9. Drop off donated items

10. Make plans for the items you want to sell

      a. Set a date for a garage sale

      b. Call a consignment shop

      c. List them on eBay

Projected Date of Completion: October 1

From this action plan you will want start adding things to your shopping list and to-do

Running Smoothly

list towards getting it done. Make a time schedule by working backwards from your estimated date of completion, leaving yourself plenty of extra time, reserving blocks of time out of your schedule to work on the project. Do not just make a mental note; write it down as if it were a set appointment. As you work your way towards completion, you will have to re-evaluate your deadline, materials, and expectations. If you are keeping to your time schedule and feel like you are not on target for your completion date, do not be afraid to give yourself an extension. (Failure to work is not an excuse for an extension! You'll just feel guilty. But do be realistic, and try not to beat yourself up.) Lastly, do something to reward yourself when you are complete. If you were resourceful enough to get the family involved, plan a fun family outing!

I think every house needs a label maker. There is just something about a printed label versus a handwritten one. I must have been a doctor in a past life, because my handwriting is terrible. It is a letdown to spend your valuable time on a project only to have it still look messy in the end because the labels are sloppy. A label maker can make even the simplest system look professional. And the better you feel about a completed project, the more likely you are to maintain it.

THE HOME OFFICE: SUPPORT WHERE YOU NEED IT

A home office is becoming more and more common for both moms and dads. One of the blessings of having a home office is that you are there to respond to life's little—or big— emergencies. Once, I was on the phone doing an important interview that could translate into some great publicity. My son had a friend over, and I was using the cordless phone so that I could sit at the kitchen table and watch them on the trampoline. Midway through answering a question, I heard that bloody murder scream every parent dreads, the one that can only mean one thing—someone is hurt. The friend came to the sliding door with blood running from his mouth. Needless to say, the interview was suspended. But you know what? The friend got taken care of, the interview got rescheduled, and it all turned out great.

Rules of Access

There is nothing more frustrating than being on an important business phone call and having one or more of your children repeating "Mom, Mom, Mom" twenty times. If you need uninterrupted time for business phone calls or to concentrate on a job, set rules of engagement for the rest of your family, and make sure everybody knows and agrees to the rules.

233 **Enlist your family's aid in deciding what hours you'll be able to work without interruption.** Check in periodically and make sure it's working for everyone (yourself included).

234 **Our rule is that, if I do not answer you by the second time you call me, assume I am on the phone** and will get with you as soon as I am done. The exception, of course, is in case of emergency—especially if there is bleeding involved.

Fearless Filing

Everyone should have some sort of a filing system for incoming papers, notes, bills, and correspondence. I use the term filing system loosely. Consider your organizing personality and make a system that fits *you*.

235 **An accordion file with monthly tabs is one simple way to file monthly bills after they have been paid.**

236 If filing by month is a little too loose for you, **you can file by category:** household, credit cards, utilities, entertainment, etc.

237

If you can and will maintain it, **creating files for each company and municipality makes it easy if you need to find past bills.** (Since this has happened only infrequently, I usually opt for a simpler way.)

238

Completely clear your desk once a week. Once a month, purge papers you have put into temporary files. Move papers to more permanent storage after a year if you feel you will need to reference them at a later date. Such items might include phone lists and/or directories, maintenance and use manuals for appliances and other household items, or things with sentimental significance. Most everything else can and should be pitched. If the information is something you might need but could look up again if necessary, it doesn't need to be taking up room in long-term storage.

Computer Stuff

Computers have become an essential tool in many families. Just as we want to make sure that we do regular maintenance on our cars and general household, we need to keep up with our computer's needs.

239 **Clean up the hard drive on your computer.** Delete files that you no longer need. (I found I still had some of Kyle's school reports from a couple of years ago.)

240 **Clean out your email spam folder.** Consult your manual about deleting cookies, temporary internet files, and history. Some highly secure sites will not let you in until you have cleaned these up.

241 What do you do when you have to move the computer and unplug all those wires in the back? The thought of getting everything plugged back in properly can be downright intimidating. Most newer computers use a very simple color-coded system—the blue plug goes into the blue receptacle, etc. **If you have an older computer or a brand that does not color code, use nail polish to color code for yourself!** With all the wires still connected, dab each plug and receptacle with their own unique color.

To Email or Not to Email?

From the "always be willing to change file": I

resisted the email craze in the beginning. I like talking to people. What doesn't work so well is when what should have been a two-minute phone call turns into a half-hour chat. I now use email instead of a phone call whenever possible for topic specific communications.

242

If you need a specific answer to a specific question, email. You can always chat at a later time.

DRESSING FOR SUCCESS: THE NO-BRAINER APPROACH TO CLOTHING YOURSELF

Let's face it; we all have to get dressed in the morning. Whether you work outside the home or not, there are a few tricks to making the job as effortless as possible.

Dressing for Success at Home

You wouldn't think of going to your job as an executive in sweats, or your job as a childcare worker in a suit and heels! The challenge at home is that our "job" changes by the hour, if not the minute. Even my most comfortable jeans are not comfortable when I am cleaning house! My favorite white shirt is not the best choice for preparing and eating meals.

243

Take a look at your day and what you hope to accomplish. If you can find one outfit that will accommodate all your activities, great! If not, mix and match tops and bottoms so that you do not have to make a complete change.

244

Never create more work for yourself. There is no reason to wash clothes that have only been worn for a short time in a "clean" environment. You can designate a shelf or set of hooks for "partially worn" clothes.

How to Wake Up Happy

The more you do at night, the more you'll enjoy your mornings, I promise. I am one of those people that actually likes mornings, but I like them even better when I can wake up feeling prepared for the day instead of attacked by it. When you take these few extra steps at night it might not seem like a big deal, but in the morning not only will you get out the door earlier and in a better mood, but chances are you will look better, too!

245 **If your schedule requires more than jeans or sweats** (my home office is very casual) **set out and iron what you intend to wear the next day.** It doesn't really take that long, and it's so worth it. Once you get in the habit, you'll never want to go back.

246 **Don't forget accessories.** It is amazing how one earring always comes up missing in the morning when you are feeling the time pressure! Or you realize how scuffed up your shoes are!

247 **This is a great habit to teach to other family members, too.** Help your kids as long as they need it, but then let them take over responsibility for their own stuff.

REDUCING CLUTTER: MAKING SPACE TO BREATHE EASY

Not to be overly dramatic, but clutter is like a cancer. It is destructive, and seems to grow with a life of its own. We become paralyzed and finally consumed by our clutter. AAARGHH!

Don't despair—it is possible to keep clutter at bay! There are two types of clutter: mental and physical. All of the ideas in this book are geared toward creating systems that will reduce your mental clutter, and chapter 1 gives you some specific planning tools for that purpose. This section will help you deal with the physical clutter in your life.

Where Does It Come From?

The problem with physical clutter is that it sneaks up on you, especially if you have lived in the same location for several years. We all have things in our home that are there just because: we don't know what else to do with it, we think someday we may actually take it out of the package, it was on sale...

248

Look around your house. What does your clutter consist of? Things you actually use, or things you are afraid to get rid of? If you have something you are not using and think someone else could benefit from it, pass it on! Give it to a friend, donate it to a church or school, drop it off at a thrift shop. You'll feel so much better having cleared the decks, and you've done some good, too.

249

The holidays are a great time to purge. What is collecting dust with little use and even less sentimental value? What would you rather get rid of than dust again? As you are rearranging your home to set out decorations, consider each item you move or put away. Do you really want to keep it, store it, deal with it any longer—or is it time to donate or consign it?

250

Avoid bringing new clutter into your house! Take two items out for every one brought in!

Out of Sight Works Wonders

If all else fails in your efforts to de-clutter, allow yourself a one-year cooling off period.

This cooling off time is a clever means of mental preparation for letting things go—but the work starts now! In order to do this, you need to follow strictly some very specific rules, as follows.

251 **Take all the items you know you "should" get rid of, but just cannot bring yourself to the point of no return, and put them in a box.** The larger your organizing project, the bigger the box—and you might need more than one. Tape the boxes shut and write the date on the outside. Put the boxes someplace where they will be out of sight and out of mind.

252 **If a box sits in storage for a year and you haven't gone looking for anything in that box, donate it—unopened!** Resist the temptation

to try and remember what you put in it. Without opening it, take the box as soon as possible to the nearest donation center. If you still cannot bring yourself to do it, ask a friend to do it for you.

Identify Barriers

Most of the time, we all have the best of intentions about putting things away after we have used them. And, as with many things in life, the smallest barriers can thwart even the strongest intentions.

253

In order to make a plan to remove the barriers, it helps to **identify what those barriers are.** What's the issue: time, not knowing where things go, reluctance to take a few extra steps?

254 Sometimes just identifying the barriers is enough to make clear what needs to happen to solve the issue at hand. Take it a step further: **How can you eliminate the barrier altogether so that it doesn't stall you, or another family member, the next time?**

255 **You can learn a lot by evaluating where things end up and why.** Is it actually a more logical place than its current home? Can you place a basket or box at the location to corral the dumped items? A container gives you a visual prompt for taking action.

Everything in Its Place

Make the most effective use of traffic patterns within your house. Train yourself and your

Running Smoothly

family to look at one another as transport vehicles as you move around the house. Scan a room as you leave it; is there something you could put away en route to your destination? In the morning, are there clothes that you could drop off in the laundry room on your way to the kitchen? Is there a glass you could take to the kitchen on your way to the bathroom? Take it one step further and put the glass right into the dishwasher instead of leaving it on the counter or in the sink.

256

Set an example for your family. Before you leave a room, survey it to find something that needs to be put away, and take it with you as you go! Once you have established the habit, start enlisting your family's aid. "Kyle, are you going to the kitchen? Can you please take that empty soda can with you?" Consistent, gentle reminders can go a long way toward establishing routine and forming habits without nagging.

257 **Better yet, put things away where they belong the first time.** Moving things from one location to another with no particular purpose fools you into thinking you did something while you actually have accomplished nothing. Remember this useful acronym from the organizing business: OHIO—Only Handle It Once.

258 It seems like everything requires an adapter: cell phone, Game Boy, laptop, Leapster, digital camera, remote control car, MP3 player. Some adapters are more universal than others. Many are exclusive to the gadget they came with. **Keep a basket or box of old or extra adapters.** They don't have to be in view but should be readily accessible when you are in a jam!

Sort It with Color

The trouble with paper is that, for the most part, it all looks alike! School papers get mixed in with junk mail, and pretty soon the field trip permission slip has been thrown in the garbage. With our busy schedules we need to be able to find and decipher information at a quick glance.

259 **Create an in/out box for each person in the house.** Sort school papers and mail near the boxes and file things immediately as they come in.

Use colored binder clips to prioritize papers that require action: a red clip for papers that are urgent or require an immediate response, a yellow clip for papers that need to be reviewed but do not have a specific deadline, and green for papers that require no action, but need to be moved to a permanent file.

Dealing with School Stuff

Here are some more ideas for dealing with all those papers that come in the door on a daily basis.

261 **Purchase a monthly accordion file at the beginning of the school year** to organize all the papers, notes, and letters that come home from school. You can keep this in your home

Running Smoothly

260

office, by a desk or worktable in the kitchen, in a wall-mounted filing pocket in the hall—just be sure it's handy.

262 Using your trusty label maker, cover up the months on the accordion file with categories that apply to your family. Some examples include: Return to School, School Information to Keep, Current Spelling List and/or Study Sheets, School Schedule, Extra Curricular Activities (schedules, permission slips, and releases). If you like, you can color code your labels, making a set of headings for each of your children.

263 An alternative to the accordion file is to **use color file folders to separate**

your family's papers. Assign each family member a color. (If you are really into detail, use the same color to write entries for that person on your family calendar.) Make files for basic categories that will be useful for all family members (e.g., Requires Action, Schedules and Invitations, Directories, Hold to File). Keep these common files in the same order in the front of each family member's section. Then make files specific to the individual as necessary that will go behind this core. If you pull out a file, return it to the same relative location to make them easy to find.

Running Smoothly

264 Go through files once a week with your children, get rid of what is no longer needed, and permanently file the items you want to keep but no longer need close at hand.

You've Got Mail

I wonder how much money is spent sending junk mail each year? Establish a routine for handling the mail. Sort it as soon as possible once it is in the house.

265 With the growing prevalence of identify theft, you should consider having a shredder for disposing of sensitive information. Shred credit card offers and any personal financial information such as bank statements. I like to accrue items for shredding and then tackle it all at once. This way I can keep the shredder put away until I need it.

266 Toss junk mail that does not have personal information and does not need to be sent through the shredder.

267 **File bills and other correspondence into the appropriate files or locations.**

Carried Away with Catalogs

I sometimes get frazzled by the amount of paper my children bring home from school, but if I take a serious look around I see that their contribution is minor compared to the magazines, catalogs, and newspapers we bring in! My old mail carrier swore I got more catalogs than anyone else in my zip code!

268 **Make a plan for the storage or disposal of periodicals.** I try to discipline myself. If I know there is nothing I "need," I dispose of it quickly—before I change my mind!

269

There is no need to keep a two-hundred-page catalog for one page of information or one photograph. **Use a three-ring binder to collect and organize information you want to keep from magazines and newspapers.** Make a few broad categories—home, school, health, etc.—and tape or paste the articles on the pages, with tabbed dividers between sections. If you are more technologically advanced, you can scan them to save on your computer.

Don't Let the News Get You Down

Newspapers have from time to time been an issue for my husband and me. Once they are read, I figure we are done with them—right? Wrong! He likes to know that he can go back and look something up a couple of days later.

270 We have a "holding basket" where each edition of the newspaper goes for its wait-ing period before recycling! (I have to admit, it has come in handy when I've needed packing for a shipment and run out of bubble wrap.)

No Piles, Ever!

Left without controls, piles of paper have a ten-dency to grow to levels that become increas-ingly intimidating, not to mention an eyesore.

271 Try using large manila envelopes or boxes in areas of the home where papers tend to pile up. When the box or envelope is full, you will know a purge is necessary. Since an envelope only holds so much, the limited space will be a built-in trigger for action.

Better Junk

Don't you hate it when your words come back at you through your child's mouth? Looking for something in my son's room the other day, I came upon a drawer that was a tangled mess of small toys, coins, and cords. When I suggested he clean it out, he informed me that "everyone needs to have a junk drawer." Of course he is right—a quick dumping place is useful—but what good is a junk drawer if you cannot find anything in it! Even your junk drawer can work better for you.

272 **Clean up your junk drawer using a silverware tray and small jars or boxes** to keep items sorted. Find a permanent home for items that are not of immediate use.

273 Leave one box or area of the drawer for those items you need to toss in on the go. As the area fills up, sort through and move the items to a more orderly home.

Double Take

Multitasking isn't just for you—why not have everything in your house function as cleverly and efficiently as possible? Look for furniture and other household items that have multiple uses.

274 An ottoman with storage inside is a great place for blankets, throws, or even kids' toys.

275 Wipe out a couple of laundry baskets to help carry presents to and from Christmas parties.

Running Smoothly

276 **Be creative**—think of new ways to use what you have in the house before you go out and buy more stuff.

277 **Try not to purchase things that have a very limited use.**

Practical Can Be Pretty

It is not uncommon for me to pick up on a trend on its way out. I bought my first pair of bootleg jeans just as the rest of the world was going to the wide leg. Well, I've just caught on to something my friends tell me has been around for a while. Have you seen those cigar box-style purses? They are beautiful, but for my life in Kalamazoo, not very practical for their intended use.

278

Cigar box purses *do* work and look great for holding makeup and hair products on the bathroom counter. They look like decorative pieces, yet they keep what I need close at hand. **Take a look around your house—even pretty things can have a function beyond their intended use!**

FEEL-GOOD PROJECTS: SAVE IT FOR A RAINY DAY

Family Photo Marathon

For those of us who are scrapbook impaired, what to do with family photos can be a source of much frustration. Here's a great rainy day project for you and as many family members as would like to be involved. (Of course, if you are the one taking on this job, you have the right to destroy any photos of yourself that you would not want to get into the wrong hands.) The theme for this activity is SORT–TOSS–STORE.

279 Sit down with all your photos. Have a basket or box for each member of the family and another box for miscellaneous photos. **Sort the photos according to family member.** (If you prefer you can choose any categories that make sense to you—such as Vacations, School Functions, Holidays, etc.—as long as you don't have too many.)

280 **Toss extra prints that you do not need** and shots that you still can't figure what you were aiming at.

281 Once all the pictures have been put into the appropriate boxes, **set some time aside to start putting them in chronological order and writing quick notes on the back** identifying who is in the picture and when it was taken. Use a marker or pen specially made for writing on photos.

282 With the photos sorted, in order and identified, you may even get the bug to do **something creative with them!** That scrapbooking thing really is kind of fun...

Rotating Gallery

I love to have pictures of my family displayed around the house, but it's possible to get into a rut.

283 Go through your recent photos and pick a few of your favorites. **Replace the old photos you have on display with these new, up-to-date ones.**

284 You can file the photos you removed from the frames until it's time for another rainy-day photo sort. Or, if you find you miss having them up, you can rotate them back into the frames.

285 It's fun to shop for frames; just keep in mind that **even very personal items can become clutter if we overdo it.** Those pictures of your beautiful family need to be dusted! Only you can decide how much is too much and keep the balance that works for your home.

MEAL PLANNING, GROCERIES, AND SHOPPING: HEALTHY FOOD AND HAPPY EATERS

Meal planning is a great tool for families on many levels: it saves money at the grocery store, eliminates last minute stress when putting dinner on the table, leads to less eating out (again saving money), and is a great way to get the family involved.

Making a List

Preplanning meals will produce a much more targeted grocery list. It also eliminates purchasing multiples. I know if I do not go to the store with a list, I will purchase items I do not need and end up with four bottles of vanilla on the shelf!

286 **Plan a week's worth of meals,** then, looking at your menus, determine what ingredients you already have in the house and put the rest on your grocery list.

287 Make a list of the stores where you like to shop for certain things: discount clubs, local grocer, other specialty stores. **Make your grocery list according to store.**

288 **Write your grocery list to roughly match your store's layout:** produce first, dairy last, etc.

Get the Family in the Act

Getting the family involved can take a lot of pressure off the primary cook. Cooking is usually the easy part. Coming up with ideas is much more stressful.

289

Assign each member of the family a night that they are responsible for the menu and helping with preparation. Younger children may need extra assistance, but what a great learning opportunity!

290

Take it a step further and challenge your family to plan meals under a certain dollar figure. This is a great way to educate the whole family about what things cost and raise their level of appreciation.

The Master Plan

A more structured approach to menu planning is to create a four-week rotating schedule. Once this is in place it can really make meal planning a breeze. My cooking skills are less than gourmet; luckily my family is not particularly picky or discriminating. We have a core set of meals that we eat on a regular basis. I try to keep key ingredients on hand at all times.

291

Make one grocery list of ingredients that can be purchased at the beginning of the month without risk of spoiling. **Purchase as many things as you can ahead, and in bulk if possible, to save money.**

292

At the same time that you are making your master list, **make four separate weekly grocery lists for those items you will need to purchase fresh for that week's meals.** Keep the grocery list for the coming week close at hand so that you can add snacks, staples, and other miscellaneous items.

293

If a month seems a little too much to plan all at once, try using rotating weekly menu plans. Create four or five weekly menus along with corresponding grocery lists, and just pull the one that fits your taste and schedule best for the coming week.

Take-Out Time

294

Keep a file of your favorite take-out restaurant menus. As you come across coupons in the mail or newspaper, clip them to the appropriate menu to make sure you do not forget to use them.

295

Put the menus with coupons nearing their expiration date at the front of your take-out menu file. If you do not have your heart set on a particular type of meal, order from the restaurant whose menu is at the front.

The Frugal Shopper

There are plently of good reasons to be frugal when you shop: practices such as buying in bulk are not only good for your budget, they help conserve natural resources by cutting down on excess packaging.

296 If you can, buy your favorite soaps and cleaners in gallon sizes and transfer into smaller, reusable bottles.

297 Now that I have sufficient storage, I like to buy as many things as I can in bulk and will sometimes buy extra when they are on sale.

298 Keep track of the price of items at the various stores you visit and make a note of where commonly purchased items cost the least; with a little planning, you can make sure you're not overspending.

299

Treat yourself to little splurges, especially when they make a mundane task more pleasant. Take, for instance, dishwashing liquid. I have gotten hooked on a brand that is made with *fresh* (how fresh can dish soap be?) lemon verbena. The deal was closed by the fact that it also comes in a pretty bottle. Remember, buying a cheaper version doesn't make sense if you don't like it and won't use it.

Don't Forget the Card

Arriving back from a family vacation, some serious grocery shopping was in order. I was headed to the discount club first, then on to our local grocery store for some specialty items. What I had forgotten was that I had cleaned out my wallet before vacation, safely putting away any items I would not need for the trip—my discount club membership card included! Here's how I could have avoided this annoying episode.

300 Using a hole punch, make a hole in the corner of all your reward and membership cards. Put all the cards onto a binder ring, which can be purchased in a variety of sizes at any office supply store. *Don't* include any cards associated with a credit line, as it may not be totally secure. Keep your card ring in your car's console or glove compartment. If you want to make an unexpected stop, you will have the card you need close at hand!

THE CAR: YOUR MINI HOME ON WHEELS

I love to drive! My father was in the automotive industry, so you might say that I come by it honestly. I love the gadgets, options, and features that today's vehicles offer. Navigation systems, DVDs, MP3s—it's like driving your home entertainment center!

But here's the thing—when I am in the car with my family, I want to feel that we're spending time *together*. I figure I have a captive audience! No earphones or Game Boys here. We are planning a family trip to Washington, D.C. My son is having a hard time comprehending that we will be spending that much time in the car with no entertainment—except, of course, for each other.

Considering how much time you spend in it, you and your family deserve to have your car be as clean, comfortable, and functional as the rest of your living environments. All it takes is a little bit of set-up.

Car Survival Kit

301 Use a lunchbox, old briefcase, or other creatively recycled container to organize a collection of items to keep in your car for meeting a variety of life's little circumstances.

- Extra batteries for toys and flashlights
- Over-the-counter medications for everyday ills
- Hairbrush, comb, and a small spray bottle of water (Am I the only parent who has had days when you get to school and realize that no one brushed their hair?)
- Moist wipes for dirty hands and faces
- Note pad and pen for making lists while stuck in traffic or writing a last-minute note for school.
- Phone list of emergency contacts: doctor, dentist, hospital, etc.

- Disposable camera. Great for capturing spontaneous moments with the kids—or documenting something less pleasant, such as a minor accident, for the insurance company.
- Small packs of vinyl and glass cleaning wipes. Keep these under your front seat for quick cleanups while you are waiting for practice to end.

Glove Compartment

302 **Give your glove compartment a checkup.** It can be handy for storage, but you do want to keep it uncluttered enough that you can find what you need.

303 **Make sure you have all necessary documents ready at hand.** Needing them is

stressful enough, without not being able to find them! Keep these items together in a Ziploc bag or folder to make sure they do not get lost in the shuffle.

- Car registration
- Proof of insurance
- Vehicle owner's manual

TIME FOR GENEROSITY: CARDS AND GIFT-GIVING

Having a little organization in your life can free you to be generous and do all those little things you like to do to make other people feel special.

Free to be Generous

304

Compile a comprehensive list of birthdays, anniversaries, and other important

dates you want to recognize. Each year when you purchase your calendar, use this list to fill in birthdays and other special dates.

305 Take this one step further and **set triggers in your calendar or organizer that will act as reminders.** Write a reminder the week before the special date to send a card, mail a present, or plan a special menu.

306 Take your list to the card store and purchase a card for each occasion for which you know you will want to give one. Make sure to allow yourself plenty of time at the store—card shopping in bulk is fun, but it can take awhile.

307 **Store the cards in chronological order in a box or envelope.** If you are pretty sure the recipients will not be moving, address and stamp the envelopes (check for any upcoming rate increases online or with your local post office). Do not seal the envelope, so that you can include a personal message before sending it out.

308 **Keep your master birthday list in a secure place** that you are sure to remember. Since you might only need it once a year, it would be easy to forget where you put it. If you think you will have trouble remembering, make a note on the last month of your current calendar.

Running Smoothly

On a Moment's Notice

I love to get a card in the mail unexpectedly. And although it can be challenging if I'm not prepared, I love to be able to return the favor. If you *are* prepared, when your out-of-town friends call and mention that their family pet has passed, within a few days you can brighten their day with a condolence card. It feels great to be able to send one out on a moment's notice, and it means so much to people.

309 **The trick is to go to the card store when you have time to browse;** there always seem to be cards that say exactly what you would in the same situation. Find the ones you love and that express your personality.

310 Keep a general assortment of greeting cards on hand, filed according to occasion.

311 Make sure you have plenty of stamps on hand; remember that some novelty cards require additional postage.

312 Fill an envelope with miscellaneous occasion cards, blank note cards, a pen, and stamps, and keep it in the car. When you have a few minutes waiting for the kids, you can use the time to write someone a note or get that last-minute birthday card out.

Some Gifty Tricks

I love to give gifts. But I hate feeling pressured to run out and grab something—anything—

just to say, "I thought of you...at the last minute."

313

Organize your gift ideas and purchases. Keep a running list as things pop into your head, or you see something in a store or catalog that reminds you of someone special.

314

If you buy gifts as you go, keep a gift log where you record what you bought and who it is for. When it is out of sight and out of mind, that gift is easily forgotten.

I learned this the hard way (naturally). I found a great carved, wooden sign at an art fair, which I knew my Dad would love—it was about hunting. I made the purchase, lugged it around in ninety-five-plus-degree heat, and placed it safely in the closet at home. This was June. His birthday is in early November. In late November I discovered the sign still there when I went into the closet for something else. Oh well, Christmas was right around the corner, one less thing I would have to buy. In March, packing to move, what did I find but that sign still aging nicely in the closet! Finally, almost one year later, the perfect Father's Day gift was delivered!

The Word from
the Front Lines

For me, this book has never been about imparting top-secret information that would change the world—mostly because I don't possess such information. This book *is* about sharing small ideas, concepts, and tips that have helped my family, friends, and me. We set up playgroups and send our children to preschool to teach them how to share, yet, as parents, we forget to share the good ideas we have discovered with one another. It is not that we do not want others to know. It really has more to do with self-confidence—we assume everyone else is doing it better than we are, so why would they need to know what we do? In my experience, this is clearly not the case. Everyone has something to share for the enrichment of all.

Knowing this, I set up a survey on my website to encourage people to share their views and experiences. I have thoroughly enjoyed reading your surveys and was moved by your responses and the solidarity that exists among us. It is amazing how isolated you can feel amid the chaos of a fast-paced life. This feeling of isolation breeds the self-doubt that often plagues us as parents. As you read some of the following responses, I hope you will find support, encouragement, and inspiration for your unique circumstances.

"Patience" is the word that probably appeared most frequently in the survey, occasionally as a "best attribute," fairly consistently as a "worst attribute," but most frequently in "do-overs" and "parents we admire." Our perceptions of patience are a lot like our perceptions of money: no matter how much we have, we always think we could use just a little more. We tend to base our judgments about others' patience on outside appearances, but patience really is a moving target. We all have good days and bad days, and we dread being caught during the latter. I wish we could learn to accept our weak moments gracefully—what a good example that would be for others!

Learning and growth came up a lot—surprisingly, referring more often to ourselves than our kids! If we understand and appreciate that being a parent is an ever-evolving process, why are we so critical of the mistakes we make? Every mistake is an excellent opportunity to

The Front Lines

grow and model for our kids—and even other parents—how to accept responsibility without assassinating our character. Growth is a positive experience that is often precipitated by an uncomfortable event. As so many of you so accurately described, mistakes, and the growth that comes from them, become easier to swallow with a good sense of humor. We all need to be able to laugh at ourselves.

The things that surprised most of us about being parents, will probably come as no surprise. We are all surprised by how tired, busy, and sleep-deprived we can be while still experiencing a love that was unimaginable before we had kids. That love can pour out in good times and bad, so unconditionally that it is beyond our comprehension.

The most embarrassing moments as a parent surprised me. There are many good stories of children and their mishaps, but many are about parents who spoke or reacted on impulse. Sometimes, we were our own victims, but we felt worse when somebody else got it. Even worse was being embarrassed when our children were present.

Most of us did a good job of ignoring any misguided advice we were given about parenting, but it is apparent from the responses that the good advice is often a lifesaver and keeps us grounded in the basics of life. Could it be that we have made being a parent too difficult with the proliferation of books, videos, and talk shows?

Closing the survey with the question about who you most admire provided a wonderful summary. We admire others for their sense of humor, their patience, and their love—qualities we tend to overlook in ourselves, yet are so desperate to find in others.

The Front Lines

WHAT IS YOUR BEST ATTRIBUTE AS A PARENT?

I make time for each of my children, to make them feel special. —*Kim, Kentucky*

•

My sense of humor—it helps me not to let things bother me, because if you do not laugh, you would have to cry. Being a parent is hard work, and sometimes it can be frustrating.
—*Amy, Utah*

•

I like to have fun. I like seeing things through my children's eyes. They come up with the funniest sayings! —*Jennifer, California*

•

I am not afraid to apologize to my kids when I am wrong or I have been out of line with them. Kids are smart—they know we're not perfect, so there is no reason to pretend that we don't make mistakes. —*Jacqui, Virginia*

I think my best attribute as a parent, being the mother of three busy boys, is the ability to adapt to an ever-changing schedule. No matter how organized I think I am, someone inevitably throws in an extra practice, doctor's appointment, etc. —*Gigi, Ohio*

•

My best attribute is that I am not afraid to put down what I am doing in order to spend a quality moment with my five- or two-year-old son. —*Val, Georgia*

•

Patience! Remember when your little ones just started walking and they had to move more slowly than ketchup out of a new glass bottle? It used to clench up my stomach to let them just mosey along without a care in the world, with my brain screaming, "Come on, we have to get the mail!" while my mouth was saying, "Yes, sweetie, that is the neatest dead grasshopper I have ever seen." Now, *they* are the ones

The Front Lines

that are telling *me* to hurry up, and I am just lagging behind, wishing that a dead grasshopper could stop them in their tracks like it did when they were young. —*Shannon, Florida*

•

As the children have gotten older, I have learned patience from them. I take more time to stop and listen to what they are really saying and what they really need. —*Daniella, California*

•

I know and trust that every crisis or disaster will work out. —*Colleen, District of Columbia*

•

My best attribute as a parent is the ability to think like a child and think of ideas that will make my child happy. I find special things my son likes and we find ways to explore those subjects (e.g., visiting a farm)—we rent a video and get a library book about farms. I enjoy it as much as he does. —*Stephanie, Ohio*

I enjoy life experiences, like vacations, museums, plays, parks, etc., and want my children to enjoy them as well. —*Sandy, Ohio*

•

Being there for my daughter in good times and bad. Taking being a parent seriously 110 percent of the time. She did not ask to be brought into this world, so, as a parent, I owe her the best childhood I can provide. —*Cheryl, Pennsylvania*

•

Every year, I improve as a parent and learn a new lesson. —*Andie, Colorado*

•

I would like to think that my best attribute as a parent would be my ability to remember what it was like to be little. I try to remember how I felt as a little girl and try to relate to my three children. —*Tyra, Missouri*

•

I think that I am still young at heart and can still enjoy playing with my children. —*Amy, Louisiana*

Knowing I am not perfect, doing the best I can every day, and always telling my daughter I love her. —*Michelle, Pennsylvania*

•

I know what is important and we do only those things. Forget all the rest. I do not drag my kids all over Kingdom Come. Some of our best memories from childhood are digging in the dirt! Relax and live life. Be passionate about what is truly important. —*Daphyne, California*

•

To be able to enjoy the simple things in life, like an "I love you" from a three-year-old. —*Catrena, Colorado*

•

One of my best attributes as a parent is being able to let go of my personal to-do list and focusing on the needs of my children, whether that be basic needs, the need for a playmate,

or the need of discipline and training.
—*Catherine, Virginia*

•

I am respectful of my children. If I bump into them accidentally, I say, "Excuse me." I use "please" and "thank you." I ask if they have "a minute to talk." I admit when I am wrong and I apologize. —*Pam, Tennessee*

•

My best attribute as a parent, is that I can say "I am sorry" to my kids. My kids know that Mommy is human and sometimes raises her voice or forgets things. I feel that my kids are learning forgiveness and empathy as a result. —*Judy, California*

•

That I have been challenged to be the best I can be. I have achieved things I did not believe possible had it not been for my children. —*Tonya, Michigan*

Seeing my children for who they really are—the good stuff and the bad, the pretty and the ugly, and loving them all the more for it. *—Dianne, Illinois*

•

I try to be their parent first, combining love and discipline; and I try to let them know that I am always there for them and that they can talk to me about anything. I also let them know that their well-being is my most important goal. *—Melissa, Ohio*

•

My willingness to listen to my children's ideas and sometimes admit that theirs are better than mine. *—Christie, North Carolina*

•

My ability to foster open communication between my children and me. *—Jenny, North Carolina*

•

Just being there when they need someone to

listen without judging them, and they know that I love them unconditionally, no matter what. —*Melissa, Kentucky*

•

I am still a kid at heart. It allows me to be silly and play with my daughter, which she enjoys. —*Julie, Virginia*

•

The ability to relax and not get stressed about things. —*Pattie, Ohio*

•

That I volunteer. I think it is important to show my children how important it is to help others. It is easy to talk the talk, but it is *so* important to walk the walk and have them see me doing it, both at school and in our community. —*Joni, Illinois*

WHAT IS YOUR WORST ATTRIBUTE AS A PARENT?

Being consistent is hard for me. —*Jennifer, California*

I wish that I had more time to volunteer at school functions like other mothers, but I am also a nurse who works full time. It is hard to not feel guilty for not being like all the other mothers! —*Gigi, Ohio*

•

I allow my house to be cluttered and not as neat as it should be. The children pick up on that and they do not pick up around the house as they should. —*Val, Georgia*

•

I can analyze things way too much! I also read too much. When my son was first born, I wore myself out by reading everything and second-guessing myself. I am getting better at just listening to my own gut reaction and going with what I know best. —*Mari, Washington*

•

I have a hard time letting things slide for playtime. I find myself putting it off because dishes need to be done or because the laundry needs folding. I know that the chores will always be around and that my children won't be children forever, but I struggle with this, nonetheless. —*Shauna, Kansas*

•

I have always hated the "wash the mouth out with soap" advice! What a great way to make your children afraid to talk to you or tell you anything. —*Shannon, Florida*

•

Patience. I have four children, and sometimes my patience is pushed to the max. Even though I may start to lose patience at times, I always look at it as a learning moment for my children and me! There are times when you will lose patience and be pushed to your max, but it is how you handle the situation that counts. —*Piper, Florida*

•

I am always five minutes late. —*Ronda, Illinois*

My attention span. Sometimes, I move on to the next thing before we have finished with the current issue or discussion. Sometimes, I fire off questions without giving my children the time to answer them. —*Audra, Florida*

•

Impatience and the tendency to stay in my comfort zone. —*Rachel, Pennsylvania*

•

I have high expectations of my children, husband, and self, which makes it difficult sometimes when we don't meet those expectations. —*Colleen, District of Columbia*

•

My temper is my worst attribute—if it is not done the way I expect, I get mad at the kids rather than letting them do it their way. —*Sandy, Ohio*

•

I do not have patience at times when I really need it. Then, I regret how I handled a situation, but my kids are very forgiving and they know that Mom also makes mistakes and needs forgiveness. —*Tammy, Minnesota*

•

Some days are better than others, but I really struggle with breaking up the fighting between my two children. I have to fight hard not to become angry and join in. —*Andie, Colorado*

•

I am too sensitive, and I tend to take it personally when my kids disobey me, throw tantrums, talk back, etc. My feelings get hurt and I react in an unconstructive way that does not help to defuse the situation. —*Jamie, Washington*

•

I believe my worst attribute is the fact that I worry constantly. The world can be such a scary place, and I worry every moment about their safety. —*Tyra, Missouri*

My worst attribute is being short-tempered and impatient. I thought that I was a patient person until I had children. —*Rebecca, Missouri*

•

Budgeting my time wisely during the day. I want to give my children 100 percent of my attention all day. Unfortunately, this does not occur, and it is hard to figure out an even balance between work, family, and housework. —*Trisha, California*

•

I am tough on my kids, sometimes *too* tough. I have to remind myself that they do not always have to live up to my expectations. —*Daphyne, California*

•

My soft spot for my children. They just look at me with their big eyes and all my anger melts away. Not too good for discipline. —*Kristeena, Wisconsin*

My lack of patience for the shortcomings of other parents. —*Paige, Oklahoma*

•

My worst attribute would have to be getting frustrated with "childish" behavior. I have to keep reminding myself that my kids are *kids*!
—*Catherine, Virginia*

•

Sometimes, I forget how hard it can be to be eleven years old and trying to figure out where I stand in the world. —*Pam, Tennessee*

•

My worst attribute as a parent is that I can be impatient. I can be patient with an acquaintance; however, I need to work on exercising the same consideration with my children.
—*Judy, California*

•

I tend to be so wrapped up in my job, housework, and getting things done that I sometimes forget to play. —*Melissa, Ohio*

The Front Lines

Not leaving enough time in my life to allow for the inevitable delays, setbacks, and obstacles that arise. —*Jenny, North Carolina*

•

I do not take enough time for myself. —*Tina, California*

•

Losing my patience when things do not get done according to my schedule. —*Debbie, Nevada*

•

Sometimes I get frustrated too quickly. I need to take a deep breath and try, try again. —*Julie, Virginia*

•

Lack of patience. In some situations, I am not as patient as I should be and do not always set a good example. I am only human; I am not always the super mom they think I am. —*Joni, Illinois*

WHAT IS THE ONE THING THAT SURPRISED YOU MOST ABOUT BEING A PARENT?

What did I do before?! My life must have been so boring! —*Linda, South Carolina*

•

How much time a new baby would take. I was so overwhelmed when my first child came home from the hospital. —*Jennifer, California*

•

How much I am like my own mom! —*Jacqui, Virginia*

•

The one thing that surprised me about being a parent was how protective I was of my babies. I found this inner strength I didn't know I had. —*Lisa, Oregon*

•

How tired I would always be! —*Angela, Texas*

How much time and effort it took to be a good parent. —*Michelle, Connecticut*

•

How difficult some of the decisions were going to be, how it tugs at your very soul. —*Diane, Texas*

•

How much my heart grew with each child that I had. I always worried about how I could love the new baby as much as the first baby, but your heart just fills with love for each new being that is brought into your life. You love them all so unconditionally. —*Piper, Florida*

•

How you can love and not stand your children at the same time! —*Julianne, Arizona*

•

How hard it would be. Wanting to provide the type of care that will create happy, well-rounded adults who will enjoy their lives, both as children and as adults. —*Audra, Florida*

I learn so much, and my capabilities grow daily. I am a better mom now than I was three years ago—it gives me hope for the future!
—*Rachel, Pennsylvania*

•

My kids always seem to know how to make me happy and put a smile on my face. We have had a difficult year, but when I look at things through the eyes of my children, I realize that they have more faith than I do sometimes. They have hugs whenever I need them, give me little treasures they have made to make me feel better, and say, "Mom, I love you to the moon." —*Tammy, Minnesota*

•

I never expected to realize that, before I had children, I was completely self-centered. I just thought I was an average person. Being a parent is a full-time giving of yourself and putting them first in every way. —*Andie, Colorado*

How much I could love someone. *—Jamie, Washington*

•

I was surprised the most by the sheer responsibility of parenting. I knew it in my head, but when I came home from the hospital with my first child, I was hit with the fact that he is mine forever, 24/7. And there are no real breaks—yeah, they may spend the night with Grandma or go to camp, but they are still on your mind and in your heart the whole time. *—Rebecca, Missouri*

•

The one thing that surprises me most about being a parent is that I did it and loved it! I always thought I would be a career woman and was shocked to discover that staying at home with my kids was the greatest job I had ever had. *—Karen, New York*

•

Laundry!!! *—Tish, North Carolina*

How difficult it would be to be consistent with discipline. Nothing is as black and white as it was before children. —*Daphyne, California*

•

The unconditional love that my two little ones give me. —*Catrena, Colorado*

•

How much work it actually was, and how little sleep I would get. Also, how expensive it is. —*Rebecca, New York*

•

The constant worry I have when they are out of sight. —*Kristeena, Wisconsin*

•

After all the promises that I would never be like my mom, I have become a clone of her. I see the iniquities and try to crush them every time they raise their ugly heads. —*Karen, Texas*

•

The thing that surprised me most about being a parent is that I loved it so much. Equally surprising was the shock as to how

much I would not accomplish in a day. —*Judy,*
California

•

How a smile from your child can change a
hard day at work into only a passing moment
in time, making it all worth it. —*Tonya,*
Michigan

•

How exhausting it is. I have not had a good
night's sleep in more than three years. —*Lisa,*
Maine

•

From their first breath, you do not get "time
off" from being a parent. It is a never-ending
job until your children are old and gray.
—*Melissa, Ohio*

•

How smart even very young children are!
—*Jenny, North Carolina*

•

I am surprised each day that—even when I am
tired, sad, mad, frustrated—just receiving a

hug or kiss from them lightens my load.
—*Christie, North Carolina*

•

What surprised me most was that the differences in how my husband and I were raised made joint decisions about how to raise our kids very challenging. —*Leslee, Missouri*

•

I am learning every day that there are over a million things that surprise me. —*Felecity, Arizona*

•

That I could love each of my daughters equally, but differently. I admire and love them each for their uniqueness. —*Debbie, Nevada*

•

How much love I had to go around, and how patient I could be. Forgetting what it was like before becoming a parent. —*Melissa, Kentucky*

How much I love my child. It is hard to imagine how deeply you can love until you have a child. —*Julie, Virginia*

WHAT WAS YOUR MOST EMBARRASSING MOMENT AS A PARENT?

One day, I asked my neighbor warily if she could hear me yelling at my boys before school in the mornings. She smiled and answered ever so politely, "Only when your garage door is up." As you can imagine, that door doesn't go up quite so early these days! —*Jacqui, Virginia*

•

My most embarrassing moment as a parent was when my three-year-old son threw a temper tantrum in the grocery store when I told him that he could not have the candy from the checkout lane. He proceeded to lie spread-eagled in front of the checkouts, screaming and crying. I ignored him, just as the "experts" say, while all of the other shoppers had to wheel their carts around him. I finished checking out, slowly wheeled my own cart around him, told him goodbye, and started out the door. My five-year-old started screaming, "Don't leave my brother." I had to go back to pick up the three-year-old and took two crying children out the door. I wanted to crawl under a rock! —*Gigi, Ohio*

•

When my almost-three-year-old son held up my sister's wedding because he needed to go potty. We were potty training very vigilantly, and he had to go right before the ceremony started. We held up the whole entrance procession until he had finished his business, because you can't start without the ring bearer. —*Shauna, Kansas*

•

One morning, I allowed my young daughter

to choose her own clothes and accessories for school. It was quite an interesting combination. She also did her own hair—and it was picture day! —*Diane, Texas*

•

When my two-year-old began breaking all the candy bars in the checkout line of the grocery store and then proceeded to start opening one and eating it! I guess he figured that they are right at his level for a reason, so why not enjoy? —*Piper, Florida*

•

Going to the grocery store with my three little boys is always embarrassing! People always say, "Boy, do you have your hands full" when what they really mean is, "Boy, I sure am glad I am not you." —*Julianne, Arizona*

•

My most embarrassing moment was when my daughter pointed out that the lady behind us in the checkout line, who had a large gap in her front teeth, was missing a tooth and wondered out loud if the tooth fairy would come. —*Rebecca, Missouri*

•

My most embarrassing moment as a parent was when my son was four, and he vomited in the doorway of a restaurant—right in front of the maître d'! —*Karen, New York*

•

In a hurry to get to church, I put my daughter's shoes on the wrong feet. Walking into church, I told her to hurry up. A lady walking past us said, "Oh, my goodness, her shoes are on the wrong feet—no wonder she is going so slow." Without thinking, I looked at her with disdain and belted out, "Well, if that is the only thing we have done wrong today, it has been a good day indeed." The lady was so surprised, and I was so embarrassed as I headed into church with my head hung low.
—*Margaret, Texas*

Standing in the produce department of the local grocery store with my two-year-old son throwing tomatoes as fast as he could. He was at the stage where he would throw everything! I was trying to stop him and catch tomatoes at the same time. —*Daphyne, California*

•

I was in a grocery store with my then-two-year-old son, and I was eight months pregnant with my second son. We passed an older, very overweight woman and he shouted out, "Look, Mommy, she has a baby in her tummy, too!" I apologized and quickly moved on. —*Gaye Lynn, Arizona*

•

This may be too much information, but it was honestly the night we learned we must begin to close the door...! —*Karen, Texas*

My most embarrassing moment as a parent was in the food court in our local mall. As I lifted my daughter into the high chair, her foot caught under my skirt. I felt a bit of a draft as my skirt lifted. —*Judy, California*

•

When my son wanted to use Mommy's "special napkins" for dinner. He had found my maxi pads earlier that day and wondered what they were. I could only come up with "Mommy's special napkins" to answer him. —*Dianne, Illinois*

•

This embarrassing moment starts with a funniest moment. We went to dinner with some close friends to an authentic Mexican restaurant with high-backed chairs. My daughter kept pushing back on the back legs of the chair and, finally, over she went with a thud! "Embarrassing" was when she did it three more times. —*Joni, Illinois*

WHAT IS THE BEST PIECE OF PARENTING ADVICE ANYONE EVER GAVE YOU?

Enjoy your children when they are young. Take advantage of the times as youngsters when they want your attention and want to be with you. It seems to fade quickly as they get older. —*Kim, Kentucky*

•

Never say, "My child will never do that," because they will. I had to learn the hard way and eat my words. —*Linda, South Carolina*

•

Do not be afraid to ask for help. —*Jacqui, Virginia*

•

The best piece of parenting advice I have been given would be the fact that, as a mom, you do not know all the answers instinctively. A lot of it is trial and error with a mix of commonsense and love. —*Lisa, Oregon*

Be consistent. —*Angela, Texas*

•

When you want your children to listen, whisper. When you feel the least loving towards your children is when they need it the most. —*Michelle, Connecticut*

•

Be consistent, whether it be with discipline, routine, or dinnertime together. —*Val, Georgia*

•

Be patient with your children. They want your approval so badly. —*Ronda, Illinois*

•

Take a nap. Let it go. Remember that these years fly and they will never come back. Savor every moment—even the messy, frustrating, "you've got to be kidding me" moments. —*Rachel, Pennsylvania*

•

Everything always works out for the best eventually. —*Colleen, District of Columbia*

The Front Lines

Have a sense of humor. —*Joanne, Florida*

•

Take time for myself and also with my husband. It is so easy not to do that and fill the time with other things, but the time spent refilling our own tank and nurturing our marital relationship is more beneficial than you realize. —*Tammy, Minnesota*

•

Do the best I can and accept that. —*Cheryl, Pennsylvania*

•

The housework can wait, but the kids cannot, so always stop first to read a book to them! —*Melissa, Illinois*

•

Before my first child was born, I read in a book that a parent should focus on being a parent and not try to be your child's best friend. That has helped me keep my focus, especially when my kids think I am being the bad guy. —*Rebecca, Missouri*

The best piece of parenting advice I got was: "The best thing you can do for your children is to love their daddy!" —*Karen, New York*

•

With kids the days are long, but the years are short. —*Tish, North Carolina*

•

Relax. No parent is ever perfect. Say you are sorry. —*Margaret, Texas*

•

Never take a day for granted, because if you do not make time for your kids, they will grow up before you know it. —*Lora, Virginia*

•

Enjoy every minute, because it goes by too quickly. —*Catrena, Colorado*

•

The work you do as a mother will last a lifetime. —*Gaye Lynn, Arizona*

Do what you feel is right for your child. Every child is different, so your parenting techniques need to differ for each of your children. —*Rebecca, New York*

•

Kiss and hug your kids morning, noon, and night—and as often as possible in between. —*Kristeena, Wisconsin*

•

Try to keep things in perspective. What seems monumental today will be forgotten completely the next. —*Paige, Oklahoma*

•

Choose your battles wisely! —*Melissa, Ohio*

•

Trust your intuition. Moms have truly been given a gift to "know" things. Once we become seasoned parents, we begin to trust ourselves more. —*Karen, Texas*

•

Never say never! —*Pam, Tennessee*

The best piece of parenting advice that I have received is to take care of myself. I notice that, if I do not do that, I cannot give as much to my family. —*Judy, California*

•

Until you have and love a child, you have not loved at all. —*Tonya, Michigan*

•

Stay organized so that life feels less chaotic. Now that I have three young kids, one with special needs, I really have to stay on top of things so that I feel in control. —*Lisa, Maine*

•

Your child will make plenty of friends. What a child needs is a parent, a guide who is caring and nurturing. —*Dianne, Illinois*

•

If you teach life's lessons while they are young, the teenage years go much more smoothly. Also, my grandma was right! —*Melissa, Ohio*

Your children do not hinder you from you work; your children *are* your work. —*Jenny, North Carolina*

•

A close friend told me to make sure I nurture their spirits, not just their minds and bodies. —*Debbie, Nevada*

•

When you say "no," you cannot change your mind—your "no" needs to mean "no." If it does not, your kids will never take you seriously. —*Melissa, Kentucky*

•

Take care of yourself—it makes you a better parent. —*Julie, Virginia*

•

Who cares if the dishes or the laundry get done? Spend time with your kids. —*My mom, Wynetta*

WHAT IS THE WORST PIECE OF ADVICE ANYONE EVER GAVE YOU?

"You can be friends and a good parent at the same time…" —*Kim, Kentucky*

•

Trust a book or advisor more than your instinct. —*Tish, North Carolina*

•

"Be your child's friend." Your job is to *parent*, and sometimes that means you will not be friends. —*Daphyne, California*

•

That regular mealtimes are not that important. The giver of this advice just let her kids eat whenever they wanted. I believe in a bit more structure. —*Debbie, Nevada*

•

Kids are flexible and forgiving no matter what you do. *Wrong*. They get their feelings hurt, too. —*Joni, Illinois*

IF PARENTS GOT DO-OVERS, WHAT IS THE ONE MOMENT AS A PARENT YOU WOULD DO OVER?

Trying to be a super mom! —*Kim, Kentucky*

•

I would spend more time just playing and laughing with my kids instead of worrying that the dishes in the sink need to be washed.
—*Amy, Utah*

•

Birth—I would have taken the epidural!
—*Linda, South Carolina*

•

Get organized before I had children.
—*Jennifer, California*

•

I would do over all the times I said negative things about my stepchildren's mother.
—*Shauna, Kansas*

A moment when I was yelling at my child for something he did not even do. —*Julianne, Arizona*

•

Reacting in anger. —*Audra, Florida*

•

My eldest son's first report card from middle school and my reaction to it. —*Colleen, District of Columbia*

•

I would spend less time worrying about housework and the details of life and more time just hanging out with the kids, looking at the sky, coloring pictures, or whatever was happening that day. Housework will be there tomorrow, but my kids grow every day and may not want to color tomorrow. —*Tammy, Minnesota*

•

I would probably put less work into our outings and spend more time enjoying them. —*Trish, Ohio*

I would go back to my first child and spend the first year of his life raising him with the confidence that I gained when I had my second child. —*Rebecca, Missouri*

•

If I could have a do-over moment as a parent, I would hold my son, who passed away, one more time. —*Karen, New York*

•

Re-evaluate my career path once I graduated from college. I should have listened to my gut feeling and followed my own dreams of a career path instead of my mother's. My outcome would have been a little different, but it would have been *my* choice. —*Trisha, California*

•

Any time when I let my schedule override the needs of my kids and, in frustration, I yell at them for not coming, helping, or obeying. —*Margaret, Texas*

My daughter overheard me talking to a friend one day as I was pouring out my frustration about her. She was only four years old, and she looked crushed. I have learned to keep my mouth shut and just bring my frustrations to God, not everyone else. —*Daphyne, California*

•

There are times when I get so frustrated that I holler. I do not like being that kind of mom, but I know sometimes you just cannot help it. —*Lora, Virginia*

•

There are too many to choose from. I try to learn from them, though, and try not to repeat them. It does let my kids know that I don't know everything and that I make some mistakes, too. —*Paige, Oklahoma*

•

I would have finished college first and *then* had my children, instead of going to college now and having less time with my kids. —*Tonya, Michigan*

When my twenty-year-old called and said he had wrecked his car, and I first asked him was the car drivable. He had gone out when I had told him not to, my husband was not at home, and I had two other children asleep in the house with no one to call to come over. Even after I explained why I had said that, he never really got over that hurt. —*Leslee, Missouri*

•

Read to them more than I have. —*Tina, California*

•

When my eldest daughter was in kinder-garten, she was getting a Citizenship Award at a special ceremony. I had the flu that day and slept right through the ceremony. Every child had a parent there except her. I really want to do that over. —*Debbie, Nevada*

•

The first time I made my girls cry because of something I did or said. —*Joni, Illinois*

WHAT IS YOUR FUNNIEST MOMENT AS A PARENT?

Letting my girls give me a "makeover," and then forgetting to clean myself up before answering the door. —*Kim, Kentucky*

•

I was in labor with my eighth baby and waiting for my husband to get home when my six-year-old daughter said, "I do not see what your problem is; you don't look like you are in that much pain." —*Amy, Utah*

•

Underestimating my momentum while demonstrating the Slip-and-Slide to my son. —*Chenoe, FPO*

•

My two little boys got naked, coated themselves with Vaseline, and then stuck coins all over their bodies. They came in and said, "Mommy look at our shields of armor!" —*Sandy, Ohio*

My daughter was only three years old and we were waiting for her pediatrician. The doctor was running about forty-five minutes to an hour late for our appointment. I made the mistake of telling my daughter that my time is just as precious as the doctor's and that I did not appreciate the idea of the doctor wasting my time in the doctor's office. Well, the doctor finally came in and asked how we were doing today. And, of course, my daughter repeated my comment to the doctor, and I turned so red that my face felt like it was going to explode. The lesson learned: to watch what I say in front of my children, especially if I want it to be confidential.
—*Trisha, California*

•

When I told my daughter that, if we did not clean up the nursery, the leader would have a cow. My daughter replied, "Wow! She will? I want to see a cow!" —*Daphyne, California*

When my son came home from his first day of kindergarten, plopped down on the couch, and said, "I'll tell you one thing, I will never do that again!" It has been an uphill battle ever since. —*Pam, Tennessee*

•

The funniest moment would have to be when I had to coax my two-year-old son (who is notorious for throwing tantrums when we have to leave) out of a party with a cookie. I used the cookie like bait and he chased me all the way out to the car. —*Judy, California*

DO YOU HAVE AN ORGANIZING TIP THAT WORKS FOR YOUR FAMILY?

Teach your children early the importance of helping with household chores. —*Kim, Kentucky*

The Front Lines

My family and I have weekly menu plans for the family with breakfast, snack, lunch, and dinner. This helps with school lunches, and the children (ages seven and nine) can get up and start helping themselves because they know what they are having for breakfast each day by looking at their lists. —*Michelle, Connecticut*

•

We have three buckets of toys, and I switch them out every week. —*Mari, Washington*

•

Each person in my family is assigned a highlighter color on our calendar. I always know with a quick glance who is scheduled for something each day. —*Shauna, Kansas*

•

Have a family calendar that sits out on the kitchen counter. We sit down as a family and add activities at the beginning of each month so that we all know what is happening that

The Front Lines

specific month. Whenever someone has something else to add, they go to the family calendar to make sure there are no scheduling conflicts, and then add it to the calendar. With four children, it is a great way to keep up with all the different directions everybody is going. —*Piper, Florida*

•

Shoe baskets by the front door, garage door, and sliding glass door. Toy buckets labeled with pictures (since my kids can't read yet). —*Julianne, Arizona*

•

Keep baskets on the stairs, next to your husband's side of the bed, in the kitchen, and anywhere else clutter gathers—it is much easier to put away. Keep containers in the kids' rooms that they can organize easily. Do a little cleaning every day and the work will not pile up—especially the laundry. Keep separate baskets for each family member. Fold the load as you remove it from the dryer and place it in the proper basket. If you only touch each piece of laundry once, you save a lot of time. The less time spent looking for things and getting things ready to go, the more time you can spend with your family. Things come and go, money comes in and goes out, but time never returns. —*Ronda, Illinois*

•

Write everything down in the family calendar. —*Colleen, District of Columbia*

•

Break up the chores into a little bit every day. A stay-at-home mom and small child do not have the time to do all the cleaning in one day. I assign different chores to different days of the week; therefore, I do not have to worry about the kitchen until it is the day to clean it (other than basic cleanup of course). —*Stephanie, Ohio*

Find a home for everything, and always return things back to their homes when finished with them. —*Joanne, Florida*

•

Each child picks one meal per week and fills it in on the calendar. They are also responsible for meal preparation on the night they picked the meal. That way, I have help in the kitchen and also quality one-on-one time with each child. We also have leftover night, which is a lifesaver for me. —*Tammy, Minnesota*

•

I stock up on ground beef and chicken when it is on sale. I brown the ground beef and freeze it in one-pound containers. It makes life so much easier when fixing meals. —*Tammy, Minnesota*

•

I have a homework corner—everything is there that is needed for homework, so we aren't spending time searching for a particular item. —*Tammy, Minnesota*

We pick out clothes for the entire week on Sunday night. No time is wasted in the mornings finding clothes. —*Tammy, Minnesota*

•

Keep your keys either in a decorative bowl or on a hook by the door. —*Tyra, Missouri*

•

Teach your kids to sort the laundry in the laundry room. I have three baskets, and the kids are learning which clothes go in which basket. This way, they can bring their baskets of laundry and sort them without dumping them all over the laundry room floor and waiting for me to do it. —*Rebecca, Missouri*

•

One organizing tip that works for us is leaving our shoes on shelves in the closet on the front porch. As we are leaving, we know exactly where to find them and they don't clutter up our inside closets! —*Karen, New York*

Teach kids simple chores (e.g., making the bed, setting table, etc.) very young and they will want to help. This makes it a habit by the time they do not want to help anymore. —*Tish, North Carolina*

•

I carry a basket in my car with coupons, scissors, and anything that needs to be dropped off or delivered. I cut out and organize coupons while in school carpool lines. —*Margaret, Texas*

•

We keep a small laundry basket with each child's name on it in the main living area. As I come across belongings and toys, I throw them in the basket. Before nap and bed, the kids take their baskets to their room. This keeps the rooms and floors free of clutter and potential hazards. —*Daphyne, California*

•

Write everything down. —*Gaye Lynn, Arizona*

Routines. My family would fall apart without some kind of routine. Meals, baths, homework, play—there is a time for everything. —*Rebecca, New York*

•

All school papers go in a tub for that school year and then, during the summer, we sort through the tub to pick out some of the favorites to keep. By then, there is much less of an emotional attachment to many of the papers and artwork. —*Catherine, Virginia*

•

A magnetic wipe-off calendar that is placed on the back door at eye level. Every family member uses their favorite color marker and is responsible for filling in their appointments. —*Pam, Tennessee*

•

We organize our toys into different bins and place a picture of the toys that are in them. My two-year-old can even help out. —*Judy, California*

Routine, routine, routine. I try to do the same things every day so it becomes a habit. —*Lisa, Maine*

•

I am a fanatic about mail—I cannot stand for my husband to open it, look at it, and then deposit it on the kitchen counter, only to remain there for the next five days. We have a large divided basket in our den (adjacent to the kitchen). As mail is opened, it is placed in the correct section of the basket depending on the type (Bill to Be Paid, Receipt for Giving, Personal Correspondence, etc). Then, at least every few weeks, I take the entire basket up to our office and file or pay bills as appropriate. This really cuts down on clutter. —*Jenny, North Carolina*

•

Just have your kids pick out what they want to wear to school the night before. Have a basket for each child to put shoes in—trust me, they will not use shoe organizers. —*Melissa, Kentucky*

What helps me is just keeping the house in order. Everything has a place and keeping the house picked up and things in that place really helps. *—Julie, Virginia*

•

If you have not used it in six months or more, toss it (or sell it). *—Wynetta, my mother*

WHO DO YOU MOST ADMIRE FOR THEIR PARENTING STYLE OR SKILLS AND WHY?

My husband—he is very patient. He spends time playing and laughing with our kids. He works hard and sets a great example for my kids to follow. *—Amy, Utah*

•

My friend, Tiffany—she lets her kids be their unique selves, not like all the other kids. She is fun and loves them unconditionally. *—Angela, Texas*

My best friend—she sees the beauty and humor in everything. —*Shauna, Kansas*

•

Good friends of ours named Scott and Kelli—they are strict when they need to be, but there is always an air of humor in their discipline (like Bill Cosby). Their children have learned to be very respectful and obedient with a smile. —*Piper, Florida*

•

My father—when my sister and I were growing up, we did not have a lot of money, but we both knew that we were loved more than anything in the world. Even though we lived in a tiny apartment, we look back now and those are some of our best memories in our whole lives. —*Daniella, California*

•

A lady in our church who has seven kids—five of them are boys—and she is always smiling and very patient. —*Julianne, Arizona*

Anyone who has more than one child and never seems out of sorts. I know a lady who has six children and whose husband is a busy doctor, so he is gone quite a bit. She stays at home with the kids, as the oldest is only twelve and the youngest is three. I have never seen her lose control. —*Ronda, Illinois*

•

My brother—he is a good role model and he tries to create well-rounded children. His children (six and seven) have good manners, show respect, and are fun to be around. He also has the ability to remain calm even when frustrated. He can tune out his surroundings and focus on his children. —*Audra, Florida*

•

My mother—she is the saint who never ever wavers. She is committed to every virtue and has never stopped striving for personal and family improvement. If I become half the mother she is, I will be a truly great mom. —*Rachel, Pennsylvania*

My friend, Angela—her kids and husband always come first. —*Colleen, District of Columbia*

•

I never thought I would say this as a kid, but now that I am a parent, I realize the wonderful way my parents raised me. They were not perfect, and neither was I, but they raised me in a loving home, disciplined me with grace, and supported me. They have been a wonderful example to me. —*Rebecca, Missouri*

•

A soccer family I know. They are obviously doing something right—it reflects in the children's attitudes towards each other and other children. They show respect and take care of one another. I am in awe every time I see them. —*Lisa, Maine*

•

I most admire women with large families who have figured out a way to "manage" their house as if it were a workplace—efficient and peaceful. —*Karen, New York*

•

My grandmothers—they had ten and nine kids each and did it without complaining. "Simplify" is their advice. —*Tish, North Carolina*

•

Amy's daughter's preschool teacher—she handles the children with such patience and grace. My daughter is a better person for having known her. —*Michelle, Pennsylvania*

•

One of my friends—she has three girls, and I have never seen her lose her cool with any of them. She really loves being a mom. She always knows a fun way to avoid tantrums. —*Lora, Virginia*

•

My sister—she is the most patient, loving, and organized person I know. She can put together a party on a moment's notice, and she has four children. I envy her sometimes, but all I can do is take her advice and do the best I can for my kids (and husband, too). —*Rebecca, New York*

•

I admire my brother and his wife because they have been really consistent with their children over the years and been firm, but loving, in their approach to discipline. They have always required the children to be respectful and kind, and now that is so much a part of their character. —*Catherine, Virginia*

•

I admire my sister-in-law, Debbie, who has a son with developmental disabilities. She always exudes love in the face of her challenges with her son. —*Judy, California*

•

I admire no one, but glean a bit from every parent I meet. —*Dianne, Illinois*

•

My mother—by respecting her and trying to follow the rules set by her, she trusted me

The Front Lines

enough to give me the freedom I needed to become who I wanted to be. —*Melissa, Ohio*

•

My friend, Genevieve, never yells. When she gets upset, she talks in the littlest voice and her kids know that they are in trouble. It seems much more productive than yelling. —*Felecity, Arizona*

•

My mom—it is amazing to see her in action with my daughter. She is a retired schoolteacher and very patient and experienced. I have said for years that "it takes Mom coming for something new to happen." Whenever my mom has visited, she has gotten Amanda to do something new, like eating solid food, learning new words, writing her name, etc. It is really a sight to behold. She has a great approach. —*Julie, Virginia*

Conclusion:
Reaping the Rewards

Getting organized is not about the process, but about enjoying the results as your house and family begin to function more efficiently. After you have finished a project or task, large or small, take at least a quick moment to savor your success. Recently, I had my husband's side of the family over for dinner. What an enjoyable time—even for me! With a little preplanning and an organized kitchen, I was able to prepare and serve the meal, as well as clean up, without missing much of the conversation. My biggest stress was what to do with the leftovers. (It is a Polish plague—we cook too much!)

I have been struck as a parent by how quickly things change—not just your kids growing up, but your perspectives, your priorities, and your passions. I used to think that "things will get easier someday when…" I have come to realize, appreciate, and—dare I say it—relish the fact that there never will be a "someday." I am not sure how our society came to believe that life is hard and it's supposed to be easy. "Easy" is a state of mind. Do I want to struggle and swim upstream, or do I want to let the current propel me to places I could not go alone, that are beyond my greatest expectations? Why do we so often choose to make things difficult?

You can have high, but realistic, expectations of yourself and your family without prioritizing those expectations above the love you share. We need to learn when to back off, when to pick ourselves up by the bootstraps or ask for an old-fashioned kick in the rear end, and, especially, when to forgive ourselves and those around us, never forgetting to make time for what's really important in life.

Every step toward an organized home is a success. There may be no parades, you may hear "thank you" only rarely, and you may even experience resistance, but in the end everyone will benefit and enjoy the fruits of your labor—having more time for what matters most. What will matter most to your family tomorrow? What matters most to you today?

INDEX

ABOUT THE AUTHOR

Amy Knapp was a businesswoman with a promotional advertising company when her daughter contracted meningitis at the age of two months. Realizing that she was going to have lifelong challenges and disabilities, Amy sold her business to become a stay-at-home mom, only to find that her organizational tools didn't help her be productive in a home environment. To fill the gap, she created *Amy Knapp's Family Organizer*, now in its sixth year with accumulated sales of over 500,000 copies. She lives in Kalamazoo, Michigan.